EMBRACE: A REVOLUTIONARY NEW HEALTHCARE SYSTEM FOR THE TWENTY-FIRST CENTURY

EMBRACE: A REVOLUTIONARY NEW HEALTHCARE SYSTEM FOR THE TWENTY-FIRST CENTURY

Gilead Lancaster, MD

www.theembraceplan.org
ISBN: 1532803966
ISBN 13: 9781532803963
Library of Congress Control Number: 2016906857
CreateSpace Independent Publishing Platform
North Charleston, South Carolina

"Of all the forms of inequality, injustice in health care is the most shocking and inhumane."

- MARTIN LUTHER KING JR. MARCH 26, 1966

This book is dedicated to Drs. Kimberly Yonkers and Charles Landau, who helped create EMBRACE, and to all the healthcare professionals who struggle in our broken healthcare system to deliver excellent compassionate care to all who need help.

Contents

Tables

Prologue

Y ou may be asking yourself, "Really? Another book about healthcare reform? Didn't Obamacare fix our healthcare system? Or ruin it?"

Regardless of your opinion of the Patient Protection and Affordable Care Act, the official name for Obamacare, it made only a small improvement to a very broken system—a system rooted in the twentieth century that is having difficulty adapting to the twenty-first. The Affordable Care Act did much to increase the number of Americans with health insurance coverage, and it possibly even reduced unneeded spending. However, it did little to address the most pernicious problems of the US healthcare system—an overly complex system that spends a huge amount of resources on treating disease rather than preventing it and that regards people differently based on their income, race, employment status, or age. Moreover, it often allows Congress, government bureaucracy, and for-profit insurance companies—rather than medical professionals—to be the decision makers.

Those who treat patients know that the problems plaguing the American healthcare system are too deep and complex to be remedied merely by revamping insurance coverage and blindly cutting the cost of service delivery. These professionals also know that the problems will only continue to fester and grow unless they are resolved. The deeply entrenched obstacles they encounter daily in their offices and their hospitals have not really been addressed by the Affordable Care Act or by the many legislative acts enacted both before and after. People from both ends of the political spectrum have come to realize that the only solution is an overhaul of the current system that will preserve its positive qualities.

EMBRACE (Expanding Medical and Behavioral Resources with Access to Care for Everyone) is a plan envisioned by a group of healthcare professionals who believe that the solution must come from those who work within the healthcare system every day, who know both its strengths and its weaknesses, and who have direct connections with the patients who use it. These professionals understand that reforming service delivery by increasing the number of insured people, or by changing the way doctors and hospitals are reimbursed, simply escalates the bureaucratic burdens and often creates misdirected incentives in patient care.

The group that developed the EMBRACE proposal, Healthcare Professionals for Healthcare Reform, concluded that the current American system is so rooted in archaic concepts, infrastructure, and technology that the only solution is to completely rebuild it. When people first hear about EMBRACE, they often have a skeptical reaction: "You mean you want to eliminate the Department of Health and Human Services, Medicare, Medicaid, and even the Food and Drug Administration?" The response is yes! When a weed with a very extensive root system overruns your garden, the only solution is to uproot the entire garden and replant it. Similarly, the only solution to our current healthcare dilemma, which has grown out of control over the past century, is to remodel it from the roots up. Of course, there may be some plants worthy of preservation, but even these may need to be replanted once the new garden is established.

You might ask, why not adopt a "single-payer" system or just expand Medicare to cover the entire population and eliminate private insurance? The answer is that both of these options are neither politically nor economically viable.[1] In 2014, private insurance accounted for one-third of national healthcare expenditures and almost 6 percent of the gross domestic product.[2] Even if Congress had the political will to go against the insurance lobby, it would be hard-pressed to find a model in any western country that does not offer some form of private insurance. Even countries with single-payer systems have developed a rather robust private insurance sector. These private payers often compete with the public system for the healthier and less "needy" patients, leaving the public sector with a patient population that is sicker and costlier to treat. These increased expenses usually lead to fewer resources and worse services, which in turn can lead to a bipartite healthcare system. Under such an arrangement, those who can afford private insurance receive efficient, full-featured services, while a slow, ineffective, expensive public system attempts to meet the needs of the majority of the population.

The single-payer models that fare best attempt to integrate the system's private insurance component into the public component in a way that reduces or eliminates competition for patients. This, in essence, is how EMBRACE is organized: as a public system that covers the basic healthcare needs of the entire population while allowing private insurance to cover what the public system does not. Instead of organizing this system as an afterthought, or as a "fix" of a single-payer model, EMBRACE merges public and private sectors into one seamless system. EMBRACE offers many incentives for private insurers—and their stockholders. Yet it significantly reduces the cost of private insurance and makes it easier for consumers to understand what they are purchasing. In addition, consumers who choose not to buy private health insurance do not run the risk of financial ruin as they do under the current system.

More important, EMBRACE modernizes healthcare in a way that brings the American system into the twenty-first century while maintaining most of the best aspects of the existing system. It is user-friendly and significantly reduces consumer concerns, such as bankruptcy or lack of coverage. However, what may be most important about EMBRACE is that it provides a system designed to deliver the best science-based healthcare to the entire US population—something that cannot be said about the current system.

This book attempts not only to explain the need for EMBRACE but also to demonstrate how it might feel to live in the United States with such a healthcare system. Working under the assumption that the reader has no background in the subject, I attempt to provide an idea of the possible effects of EMBRACE on consumers, doctors, hospitals, businesses, and even government. The book begins with a detailed general description of the plan; each subsequent chapter explains how it might benefit specific groups. Each chapter concludes with a table that compares the various features of EMBRACE to both the current system and to a single-payer system.

I include single-payer system comparison tables because it is one of the most popular alternative proposals to the current system. In addition, many people who first hear about EMBRACE often confuse it with a single-payer plan. Unfortunately, picking one such single-payer plan for the purpose of comparison is difficult; there are many different plans around the world, and there have been several single-payer system proposals for the United States. One of the most popular is the Physicians' Working Group for Single-Payer National Health Insurance (NHI), which is modeled on the Canadian healthcare system and is an extension of Medicare to the entire population.[3] Where details are lacking or unclear in the NHI proposal, the Canadian system is used.

---

1 J. Oberlander, "The Virtues and Vices of Single-Payer Health Care," *New England Journal of Medicine* 374 (2016): 1401–03. http://www.nejm.org/doi/full/10.1056/NEJMp1602009.
2 "NHE Fact Sheet," Centers for Medicare & Medicaid Services, Last Modified December 3, 2015. http://www.cms.gov/Research-Statistics-Data-and-Systems/Statistics-Trends-and-Reports/NationalHealthExpendData/NHE-Fact-Sheet.html.
3 Steffie Woolhandler et al., "Proposal of the Physicians' Working Group for Single-Payer National Health Insurance." *JAMA* 290, no. 6 (2003): 798–805.

First EMBRACE

SUMMARY OF BENEFITS

For patients/consumers:

- Provide free basic healthcare to everyone with the option to expand coverage if desired.
- Furnish a patient-friendly system with universal coverage.
- Reduce or eliminate the risk of incurring huge debt and potential bankruptcy.
- Allow fully portable coverage throughout the country.

For healthcare professionals:

- Significantly reduce bureaucratic paperwork and office overhead.
- Allow adequate time for patient care.
- Build into practice continuing medical education and maintenance of certification.

For hospitals:

- Maintain current models (community, not-for-profit, for-profit, religious-affiliation, specialty-hospital, veterans, etc.).
- Allow hospitals to predict insurance coverage and revenue.
- Significantly reduce administrative costs for billing and collections.

- Permit hospitals to have more control over the implementation and customization of electronic medical records (EMRs).
- Enable hospitals to easily acquire meaningful data about volumes and quality.

For businesses:

- Eliminate the requirement to provide healthcare insurance to employees.
- Dramatically reduce healthcare and benefit administration costs and efforts.

For government:

- Check or even reduce public expenditures on healthcare.
- Stop the impending bankruptcy of the Medicare Trust Fund.
- Eliminate the need for states to subsidize healthcare coverage (i.e., Medicaid).
- Allow Congress to control costs with one annual health budget.
- Reduce congressional involvement in healthcare policy.
- Allow "free-market" features without compromising patient health.

For private insurance companies:

- Authorize full participation of for-profit health insurance companies.
- Provide an easy-to-understand and transparent method to buy private policies.

For public health agencies:

- Improve the quality and availability of healthcare in the United States.
- Construct a healthcare system that takes advantage of twenty-first century technologies.

- Provide a mechanism to assess research needs to improve the system.
- Allow for rapid and seamless integration of practice guidelines.
- Ensure timely information regarding epidemics and other health concerns.
- Use existing infrastructure, when possible, to avoid the need to develop new, unproven methods.

If there is anything that almost everyone can agree on, it is that reforming our healthcare system is not easy. Even a relatively small attempt at reform such as the 2010 Affordable Care Act (ACA), otherwise known as Obamacare, took an incredible amount of political and social willpower. Yet it had a greater influence on healthcare spending and insurance coverage than on factors that increase the quality of and access to healthcare delivery.

Walter Cronkite, the renowned broadcast journalist, best summarized the difficulty of reforming the system when he said, "America's healthcare system is neither healthy, caring, nor a system."[4] That it is not healthy is evidenced by its relatively poor outcomes—infant death rates, maternal death rates, and low life expectancy, among others—compared to other industrialized and even some emerging countries.[5] That the system is not caring is exemplified by the large number of citizens who lack ready and affordable access to basic healthcare.[6] However, the observation that current American healthcare cannot really be called a system is one of the key reasons why reformation has been so challenging.

Unlike most other industrialized nations, over the past one hundred years, the United States has developed an incredibly complex macrocosm of private, public, and military healthcare services and insurance with no effective oversight. It has created an environment where levels of insurance and treatment are based on income, race, military service, employment status, and age rather than on severity of illness. In addition, we spend a huge amount of resources to treat diseases that the system is not really set up to prevent.

Another obstacle to reforming US healthcare is the role that government plays in it. There seems to be a significant distrust of all forms of government, especially at the federal level. There is a perception that "the government" is trying to take over and ration healthcare—and even stipulate who has access to it. This distrust has virtually paralyzed any significant lawmaking in Washington, DC, and has left many to wonder how we might be able to circumvent Congress when it comes to healthcare legislation.

However, taking healthcare decisions out of the federal government's hands would be very difficult—in fact, unconstitutional—as Congress must approve all public funding in this realm. The federal government controls the purse strings of all publicly funded healthcare (such as Medicare and Medicaid), which, in 2013, made up more than 30 percent of the US population's health insurance coverage.[7] Further, because it controls the purse strings, Congress often feels it has the right to oversee various aspects of healthcare delivery.

However, the most important reason why healthcare reform efforts are so challenging is that they are extremely difficult to understand. Much of this has to do with the intense politicization of healthcare policy and the consequent hyperbole and outright misinformation that usually result (remember "death panels"?). In addition, most people find it difficult to comprehend how any proposed changes will affect them.

Hence, the remainder of this chapter provides an overview of the proposed healthcare system called EMBRACE, and subsequent chapters explore the system's effects on various groups. If you are curious to know how the plan will affect you, the patient (also referred to as the consumer), or other groups, such as doctors, businesses, the health insurance industry, and government, feel free to skip ahead. You can always come back. If, on the other hand, you'd like to begin with an overview of the proposed system, just continue reading.

EMBRACE THE PLAN

The EMBRACE healthcare system reform plan was first introduced in the *Annals of Internal Medicine*, the medical journal of the American College of Physicians, in April 2009.[8] Around this time, the United States was in the middle of an epic political debate over reform of its healthcare system.

In general, the debate lacked the voices of those most involved in the topic and most knowledgeable about it—healthcare providers themselves. Publication of the *Annals* article appeared to be part of an effort by the medical community to enter the deliberation. But the debate among lawmakers generally ignored input from healthcare professionals and centered mostly on health insurance reform—and ultimately led to the creation of the ACA.

The ACA was a notable achievement for the estimated 20 percent of the population under age sixty-five who did not have insurance. However, even its most ardent supporters admit that it has been a relatively minor "fix" to an archaic and hopelessly dysfunctional system. Providing some level of healthcare insurance to the entire population, as the ACA attempts to do, may alleviate the most troubling aspects of the current system. However, it does little to change the outdated system itself, as is discussed in more detail in the chapter on public health.

The battle to implement the new law continues and is intensified by another presidential election. People on both sides of the debate yearn for new ideas that take advantage of the knowledge and technologies that have emerged in the twenty-first century. With this in mind, it may be time to look once again at the EMBRACE plan.

Although the plan is rooted in three innovations, all designed to work together for maximal effectiveness, each could function separately. The first innovation is a scientifically based, tiered healthcare system (the Tiered Benefits System). The second is a dedicated, unified, web-based healthcare information platform (the Healthcare Information Platform). The third innovation is a nongovernmental board led by healthcare professionals who broadly represent the entire healthcare system (the National Medical Board). I discuss each innovation separately before discussing how well they might interact.

Innovation One: The Tiered Benefits System

The Tiered Benefits System, the main pillar of EMBRACE, comprises three tiers.

- The basic level, or Tier 1, covers (1) all conditions that have been determined to be life threatening, (2) all services that have been shown to be life extending, and (3) all therapies that have been shown to prevent life-threatening conditions.
- Tier 2 covers all conditions that have been shown to affect quality of life, therapies that have been shown to improve these conditions, and services and therapies for Tier 1 conditions that lack the scientific evidence required for Tier 1 coverage.
- Tier 3 covers "luxury" services as well as other conditions not covered in Tiers 1 and 2.

Let's look at the tiers in more detail.

Tier 1. The determination of the conditions and therapies covered by any of the tiers are ultimately made by the National Medical Board (NMB), a nongovernmental agency that I discuss later in the chapter, and depends largely on scientific studies and published medical guidelines. Consequently, it is difficult to predict all of the conditions to be included in Tier 1, but heart attack, cancer, pregnancy, and severe depression are likely candidates. This tier also covers treatment of conditions that have been shown to increase the risk of developing life-threatening illnesses, such as high blood pressure, diabetes, and high cholesterol.

In addition, this tier covers all testing used to rule out a Tier 1 condition. In other words, if a patient presents to the emergency room with chest pains, Tier 1 covers any of the scientifically validated tests performed in the workup until a Tier 1 condition (like a heart attack) is diagnosed or definitively excluded. Any other testing falls under Tier 2.

Tier 2. Conditions covered by Tier 2 include those that may significantly affect quality of life but that have not been shown to affect life expectancy or increase the risk of other life-threatening conditions. These might include osteoarthritis, low back pain, and irritable bowel syndrome. In addition, this tier covers therapies for life-threatening conditions that still require scientific proof of efficacy in order to be covered in Tier 1.

In addition, Tier 2 covers testing that Tier 1 does not.

Tier 3. This tier is reserved for "luxury" treatments and procedures that have little or no scientific evidence of reducing mortality or improving quality of life, such as facelifts and LASIK surgery.

The main reason that the benefit tiers are separated is to determine coverage. Unlike single-payer systems, EMBRACE allows both public and private insurers to participate. But unlike the present system in the United States (or most single-payer systems that allow private insurance), EMBRACE separates the services each one covers. Because Tier 1 conditions are the most serious in terms of both personal and public health, they are covered by a form of public insurance. This coverage is automatic and universal and does not depend on age, gender, employment status, preexisting conditions, or even military service; it covers the entire population from cradle to grave.

Tier 2 is covered by private insurance or paid out of pocket. Like the current system in the United States, private insurance companies would be allowed to screen prospective customers when pricing policies for individuals. To reduce potential abuse (such as purchasing plans before a scheduled surgery), insurance companies might be allowed to consider some preexisting conditions when pricing a policy, as they did prior to passage of the ACA. Unlike the current system, private insurance policies must provide uniform basic offerings determined by the National Medical Board. Features and prices can be easily compared, are available in every state, and do not depend on an employer. Similar to health insurance exchanges, such as HealthCare.gov in the ACA, EMBRACE offers an online marketplace called the HealthMart, where Tier 2 insurance coverage is available for purchase directly to the public.

The EMBRACE marketplace differs significantly from the ACA. Under EMBRACE, private health insurance is primarily available for purchase through the HealthMart. Each plan is listed on a menu of offerings—something that is currently available in a limited way for Medicare recipients under what is called Medigap, a supplemental insurance policy for standard Medicare recipients (see chapter 2). The HealthMart plans must offer the minimum coverage stipulated in the menu. This allows consumers who are looking for a Tier 2 insurance plan, for example, to not only find the right one for themselves and their families but also to more easily compare prices and any additional benefits that a particular private insurance plan might offer.

Tier 2 plans may be very general or they may be very specific for particular groups, such as the elderly, veterans, or factory workers. They may be offered through supplements by the federal government (as a substitute for Medicare), Veterans Affairs (as a substitute for veteran benefits), or employers (for disability insurance or as a limited bonus).

Because Tier 2 insurance plans cover conditions and treatments that pose less of a financial risk to insurance companies, they should be significantly cheaper for the consumer than those provided in the current system yet still offer a good profit margin to insurance companies.

In most cases, Tier 3 services are not covered by any insurance, which is typical of the current system.

Innovation Two: The Healthcare Information Platform

Although the three tiers provide separate coverage, they are all overseen by a centralized platform called the Healthcare Information Platform (HIP). The HIP is a secure web-based system available to every licensed healthcare provider and is an important part of the second innovation of the EMBRACE system. On the provider side (doctor, nurse, physical therapist, hospital, nursing home, etc.), a single patient encounter page—the Universal Billing Form (UBF)—moderates all patient visits. The provider completes this form and submits it electronically to a "central computer." This computer analyzes the data and determines to which tier the patient's condition and services correspond. If a Tier 1 service is determined, the provider is paid immediately. A Tier 2 determination leads to a search for insurance and, if private insurance coverage exists, the insurance company is notified. If the patient has no insurance for a service determined to fall under a Tier 2 or Tier 3 plan, the HIP bills the patient for the service. (All Tier 1 services are covered, regardless of the patient's insurance status.)

The UBF addresses several important deficiencies in the current US healthcare system that are often overlooked when reform is discussed. The first is the inefficiency of the current billing system. Over the years, the bureaucracy that has built up around insurance billing has become one of the most burdensome and wasteful aspects of medical practice. Medical providers must either spend hours dealing with forms and discussing cases with insurance companies or hire others to do so. Although no formal numbers are available, in many doctors' offices, there are one or more full-time employees—per doctor—whose jobs consist solely of dealing with insurance companies. Other than being a burden to the doctor (or any provider), this employee adds to healthcare costs, because the provider must pay this employee's salary and benefits out of whatever he or she receives from patient services.

In addition, insurance companies spend a large amount of money and resources on the other side of the telephone to "screen" these claims. Under the current system, this screening process is an imperative part of the companies' business models and increases the cost of insurance (and, of course, increases profits). Additionally, the screening doesn't just affect the providers; it is likely that if you are a client (or a patient) with a private health insurance policy, then you have had to deal with this bureaucracy at one time or another as well. If you have not, it is likely because you have not received many services.

Billing and insurance-related activities in the US healthcare system accounted for approximately $471 billion in 2012. Much of these costs can be traced to the previously mentioned bureaucratic obstacles related to private insurance; it has been estimated that as much as $375 billion could be saved from a simplified healthcare financing system like EMBRACE.[9]

Under EMBRACE, the HIP eliminates these bureaucratic hurdles. The provider completes the UBF during the patient visit, and, based on the information entered, the HIP makes an immediate tier determination. Although the HIP's determination is final, appeals are assessed on a case-by-case basis in aggregate and periodically reviewed by the NMB to determine if the tier assignment should be changed.

In addition, the provider can request the HIP to determine the tier assignment *before* offering the service so that he or she can discuss it with the patient. If the service is determined to be non-Tier 1 (i.e., either Tier 2 or Tier 3), the patient and the provider can consider their options together. This also reduces the chance that a medical bill will surprise the consumer.

The HIP's actual web-based platform has yet to be determined (e.g., whether it would be part of the existing Internet or a "closed web"). However, access to it will be available to application developers. Much like the way the Apple iPhone and iPad platform runs Apple devices while allowing entrepreneurs to develop thousands of "apps," the HIP would be available to developers for application development that could be used by the entire healthcare system.

Apps such as EMRs (electronic medical records) are especially welcome, as many of those currently offered have the disadvantage of being incompatible with one another. These programs, which store vital patient information, must be easily accessible by a variety of medical and non-medical users who may not be working together or with the same software. This inability to freely exchange information electronically increases medical costs and adversely affects patient care.

The common platform and the stipulation that all patient data be easily accessible not only make the EMBRACE system more efficient but also provide an opportunity to obtain direct data on almost all aspects of medical care. Currently, data collection is inefficient, costly, and relatively unreliable, which makes the monitoring of routine healthcare quality difficult. As part of the EMBRACE infrastructure, the HIP allows for real-time feedback on public health programs and even the early detection of developing epidemics.

Innovation Three: The National Medical Board

Data analysis and the subsequent ability to act are difficult without a centralized agency to oversee all aspects of the nation's very large and complex healthcare system. Currently, no single agency does so, and many of the agencies or groups that do exist have duplicate "jurisdictions" that rarely cooperate. Government and nongovernmental agencies—such as the Department of Health and Human Services (HSS), the Centers for Disease Control and Prevention (CDC), the National Institutes of Health (NIH), the Food and Drug Administration (FDA), the Centers for Medicare and Medicaid Services (CMS), and Veterans Affairs (VA)—make up a complex and inefficient mosaic of healthcare oversight and services, with no clear "master plan."

Under EMBRACE, all of these agencies will either be eliminated or integrated into the NMB. This board will be comprised of mostly physicians and experts in public health and healthcare administration, as well as representatives of the pharmaceutical, business, and insurance industries. The NMB's stated mission will be to promote the health of the nation for each and every one of its citizens.

The NMB will have many functions, with its top priority being the determination of the tier assignments of various conditions and services. Initially, these tier assignments will be determined by using all available scientific evidence of testing algorithms, illness severity, and treatment effectiveness. Of course, most of the studies currently available are not designed with the intention of advancing healthcare delivery in general and EMBRACE specifically. Therefore, the NMB will eventually need to "commission" its own studies.

Pharmaceutical and medical device companies design and finance most of the large studies on therapy in an effort to obtain product approval. Consequently, the resulting information is difficult to apply to actual clinical use. Moreover, objective comparative outcome data (i.e., information on how particular drugs or devices perform against others) is virtually nonexistent. In addition, these studies often enroll limited types of patients (e.g., only patients over the age of sixty-five), so the resultant data are also limited in their clinical usefulness.

Under EMBRACE, the NMB will be authorized to commission studies designed to facilitate tier assignment specifically and ensure that the research has maximal effect on public health. As these studies are completed, the NMB will be able to "fine-tune" the various tier assignments.

The NMB will be structured similarly to the US Federal Reserve, with a physician appointed as chairperson by the president every ten years. The NMB's composition still needs to be determined but will likely include physicians and nurses; public health experts; healthcare economists; patients; and representatives of the pharmaceutical industry, device manufacturers, health insurance companies, and businesses.

The NMB will have direct oversight of the HIP. This will not only allow it to change tier assignments as information becomes available but also to provide instant access to the data generated by the HIP on diseases and therapies. These data might help the NMB to identify epidemic outbreaks early on and obtain information on the efficacy of drugs and devices long after they are approved and in public use.

Currently, information on how drugs and devices perform in the "real world" (after receiving FDA approval) is acquired through what are called Phase IV studies, which are difficult and expensive to administer. Alternatively, the FDA receives reports from doctors, hospitals, and patients regarding adverse outcomes from drugs or device malfunctions. These reports are not always reliable, and it may take time to identify a problem. Under EMBRACE, all of these data will be easily and inexpensively acquired on a constant and virtually instantaneous basis. This in turn can be quickly analyzed by the NMB and allow appropriate actions to be taken.

Although licensing for healthcare providers will likely remain with the individual states, the NMB may absorb the American Board of Medical Specialties (ABMS), which "certifies" doctors. It will then take on the task of certifying all new doctors when they finish their training. In addition, the NMB will provide various programs that help doctors maintain their clinical competency and certification. These programs will be designed to fit easily into the physician's practice with the least amount of disruption.

Funding for all NMB activities, including payment for Tier 1 services and commissioned studies, will come from an annual budgeted allowance from Congress. These funds would be raised by a payroll tax similar to—and in place of—the current Medicare funding by the Federal Insurance

Contributions Act (FICA) for consumers and a graduated tax for business-es based solely on the number of employees and their salaries.

All businesses will be taxed, but it will likely be a significantly lower expense than it is under the current arrangement, which requires employ-ers to pay for private health insurance plans. This not only reduces the financial pressures on medium- and large-size corporations but also cir-cumvents the administrative pressures of choosing and maintaining health insurance policies. This in turn significantly reduces the private sector's economic burden.

In addition, companies that offer approved workplace prevention plans to their employees receive credit on their EMBRACE-related taxes. Moreover, because the insurance is fully portable, employers do not have to earmark extra resources (time and money) for enrolling new hires. And, of course, employees do not need to stay in a particular job just to have insurance coverage.

Some businesses may want to offer an insurance "upgrade" as a form of incentive, as employers did when they offered private insurance in the 1950s and 1960s. Those that do will find that Tier 2 plans are significant-ly more affordable, comprehendible, and easier to manage than what is currently available. In addition, there are many Tier 2 categories created specifically for various professions, including those that serve as a substi-tute for workers' compensation insurance, which will be eliminated under EMBRACE.

TABLE 1. Comparison of EMBRACE, current, and single-payer systems' general features

General features	EMBRACE	Current system	Single payer†
Universal coverage	Tier 1: yes	No	Yes
Access to doctors/hospitals	Unlimited	Limited by insurance coverage	Limited by insurance coverage and geography*
Portability	Fully portable	Very limited (except original Medicare)	Fully portable
Role of employer	Tier 1: none Tier 2: voluntary	Large firm: mandatory coverage	None
Private practice/clinic	Maintain current structure	Push toward larger groups and clinics	Maintain current structure
Medical office management	Easy: little overhead	Difficult: lots of overhead	Easy: moderate overhead
Bureaucracy	Low	High	Moderate
Healthcare costs	Moderate Easy to control	Double single payer Difficult to control	Moderate Easy to control
Ease of information technology integration	Very easy Inexpensive	Very hard Very expensive	Easy Moderate expense
Healthcare funding process	Simple: one bill a year	Very cumbersome: multiple bills	Moderate: similar to Medicare
Healthcare system oversight	Strong	Weak	Strong
Public health oversight	Very strong	Fair	Moderate
Ability to integrate science-based guidelines into practice	Very strong	Weak	Strong

Note: One must keep in mind that because neither EMBRACE nor an American version of a single-payer system currently exists, some of the claims listed are best estimations.

†Because one cannot predict which single-payer model might be adopted in the United States, the NHI proposal and/or the Canadian system is used for comparison.

*Almost all single-payer systems in free-market countries have some form of private insurance that has developed separately from the original single-payer system. There are varying degrees of oversight for these plans. The independent growth of private insurance is also likely to occur if the United States adopts a single-payer model.

4   Walter Cronkite, BrainyQuote.com, xplore Inc., 2014, http://www.brainyquote. com/quotes/quotes/w/waltercron169605.html.

5   Steven A. Schroeder, "We Can Do Better—Improving the Health of the American People," *New England Journal of Medicine* 357 (2007): 1221–28, http://www.nejm. org/doi/full/10.1056/NEJMsa073350.

6   "New Health Insurance Survey: 84 Million People Were Uninsured for a Time or Underinsured in 2012; Nearly Decade-Long Trend of Rising Uninsured Rates among Young Adults Reversed," The Commonwealth Fund, April 26, 2013, http://www.commonwealthfund.org/publications/press-releases/2013/apr/ new-health-insurance-survey.

7   "Medicare and Medicaid, Age and Income," US Census Bureau, Random Samplings: The Official Blog of the US Census Bureau, September 17, 2013, http://blogs.census. gov/2013/09/17/medicare-and-medicaid-age-and-income-2.

8   Gilead I Lancaster et al., for Healthcare Professionals for Healthcare Reform, "The Expanding Medical and Behavioral Resources with Access to Care for Everyone Health Plan," *Ann Intern Med* 150, no. 7 (2009): 490–92, http://annals.org/article. aspx?articleid=744429.

9   A. Jiwani et al. "Billing and Insurance-Related Administrative Costs in United States' Health Care: Synthesis of Micro-Costing Evidence," *BMC Health Service Research* 14 (2014): 556.

2

Patients/Consumers

SUMMARY OF BENEFITS

- Free basic healthcare services from cradle to grave
- Automatic enrollment
- No out-of-pocket expenses
- Coverage for every licensed clinician and every hospital
- Basic coverage upgradable through private insurance
  - Easily comparable private plans
  - Completely transparent private policies
  - Significantly less expensive than current private plans
- Movement from job to job and state to state without loss of coverage
- Less costly (in taxes and out of pocket), regardless of income level and employment status

For years, many have anointed the American healthcare system as the "best healthcare delivery system in the world."[10, 11] This belief has endured despite convincing evidence that, when it comes to health outcomes, the US system has had mediocre results.[12, 13] Many of these unsupported claims can be ascribed to politics. Yet there may be some truth to them when it comes to patient—or, more accurately, consumer—services.

The perception is that, in the American system, it is easy to see the doctor of your choice and undergo procedures quickly. There is also the view that, unlike in other countries, there is little or no "rationing" of healthcare services. The "consumer-oriented" focus of the US healthcare system has been one of the shining lights—at least for those who have health insurance—in an extremely dysfunctional system. The potential of losing it is one of the main reasons why single-payer reform has been unpopular.

EMBRACE is specifically designed to retain as many of the good elements of the current system as possible. Many of these elements, such as the ability to see any doctor or healthcare practitioner, may actually be better than those currently available. For example, many insurance carriers now limit the number of doctors their customers can see without incurring added costs for "going out of network." Under EMBRACE, consumers have no such constraints. They can see any doctor or go to any hospital they choose, even if it is in another state.

But the real advantages of EMBRACE are its simplicity and its capacity to provide universal access to the entire population, regardless of age, gender, employment status, military service, ethnic group, income status, or ability to pay. Under EMBRACE, every US citizen is automatically enrolled (with some stipulations for noncitizens), without a fee or an enrollment form.

When EMBRACE begins, most people will be entered in Tier 1 (basic health coverage) during their first visit to a healthcare professional. All that is required on subsequent visits is a form of ID such as an identity card or even fingerprints; all information is then available to the healthcare provider through his or her computer. Newborns will be entered at birth and carry the coverage for the rest of their lives.

Although Tier 1 provides everyone with coverage of the most important and dangerous conditions, many consumers will want to supplement this "safety-net" coverage with a Tier 2 plan. Purchasing a Tier 2 plan is not mandatory, but it is likely to be significantly less expensive than private health insurance under the current system. These private plans are portable from job to job and state to state.

Those who want Tier 2 coverage can purchase it through a computer-based program modeled after the successful Medigap menu of plans. Medigap (private health insurance plans sold as a supplement to Medicare) has been working well since its introduction in the early 1990s. Its menu allows the consumer to easily compare the features of the various plans available. Table 2 is an example of the Medigap menu.

TABLE 2. Comparison of Medigap plans

Medigap benefits	Medigap plans									
	A	B	C	D	F	G	K	L	M	N
Part A coinsurance and hospital costs up to an additional 365 days after Medicare benefits are depleted	Yes	Yes	Yes	Yes	Yes	Yes	Yes	Yes	Yes	Yes
Part B coinsurance or copayment	Yes	Yes	Yes	Yes	Yes	Yes	50%	75%	Yes	Yes
Blood (first three pints)	Yes	Yes	Yes	Yes	Yes	Yes	50%	75%	Yes	Yes
Part A hospice care coinsurance or copayment	Yes	Yes	Yes	Yes	Yes	Yes	50%	75%	Yes	Yes
Skilled nursing facility care coinsurance	No	No	Yes	Yes	Yes	Yes	50%	75%	Yes	Yes
Part A deductible	No	Yes	Yes	Yes	Yes	Yes	50%	75%	50%	Yes
Part B deductible	No	No	Yes	No	Yes	No	No	No	No	No
Part B excess charges	No	No	No	No	Yes	Yes	No	No	No	No
Foreign travel exchange (up to plan limits)	No	No	Yes	Yes	Yes	Yes	No	No	Yes	Yes
Out-of-pocket limit	N/A	N/A	N/A	N/A	N/A	N/A	$4,940	$2,470	N/A	N/A

Note: "Yes" means the plan covers 100 percent of a benefit. "No" means the plan doesn't cover that benefit. "Percentage (%)" means the plan covers a percentage of the benefit. "N/A" means a certain plan is not applicable.

Source: Centers for Medicare and Medicaid Services. n.d. "How to Compare Medigap Policies," https://www.medicare.gov/supplement-other-insurance/compare-medigap/compare-medigap.html.

The rows in Table 2 represent specific features contained in the various insurance plans listed in the columns. For example, if you want a comprehensive program that covers each row, you might choose plan F; plan A offers bare-bones coverage. Once consumers have chosen the plan that best suits their needs, they can check which insurance companies offer the plan and how much it might cost.

Of course, EMBRACE offers various Tier 2 services instead of the supplements to Medicare insurance listed in Table 2. But the ability to compare plans side by side allows consumers to first find the best Tier 2 plan for their needs and then to find the best price. As with Medigap, consumers will be able to shop for plans online and verify the minimal standards of the Tier 2 plan they select.

Because Tier 1 covers most catastrophic medical occurrences, such as trauma or cancer, the price of Tier 2 services is significantly lower than that of current health insurance policies. This means that most Tier 2 plans should be affordable for the average consumer. In addition, unlike current private policies offered through a job or a healthcare exchange (either state run or federally managed plans under the ACA), any policy purchased under EMBRACE is fully portable throughout the United States.

Tier 2 plans will also be available through other means. They can be offered as hiring incentives; veteran benefits; rewards for meeting certain preventive goals (in Tier 1), such as quitting smoking or losing a certain amount of weight; or even as an age-based substitute for Medicare.

Unlike the current system, there is no need to provide proof of insurance for a doctor's visit or scheduled procedure. Instead, all insurance information is computerized and immediately available to the healthcare provider.

Finally, on average, the overall cost to consumers under EMBRACE will be equal to or less than what they currently pay. Today, most consumers pay for healthcare in many different ways—so many that it is difficult to know the true cost. There are payroll deductions for employer-provided insurance and certain health plans such as FICA (which goes to support the Medicare Trust Fund), as well as several forms of out-of-pocket payments, such as deductibles and copayments. Some insurance policies offer different coverage depending on the doctor pool, charging a penalty if the consumer goes "out of network," and premiums can change if the consumer moves or changes jobs.

Added to these direct costs to the consumer are the direct and indirect costs of the uninsured. For those who lack insurance or who may be "underinsured," the potential financial burden is tremendous. On average, the uninsured pay for more than one-third (35 percent) of their care out of pocket,[14] and they often pay higher prices for medical care than those who are insured.[15] In addition, medical debts contribute to almost half of all bankruptcies in the United States.[16]

And because many, if not most, of the uninsured often delay seeking medical care until their disease has progressed, they tend to be sicker and in need of more expensive treatment. This not only costs the patient more, but it also places a significant strain on hospital resources. State governments often supplement the financial burden hospitals incur from treating the uninsured, which, of course, means higher taxes.

EMBRACE's Tier 1 funding is simple. There is a flat payroll tax for both employer and employee (similar to what is now being charged for Medicare) at a rate determined by Congress. Although no one can predict what laws Congress will enact, we propose that the rate will be a *flat percentage* of salary and will have no upper salary limit. Therefore, people earning $1 million a year pay the same *percentage* of their annual salary as a fast-food server making minimum wage. For basic healthcare provided under Tier 1, there are no annual premiums, copayments, deductibles, or out-of-pocket payments by the consumer.

Tier 2 funding is based on how the consumer acquires the plan. Those who purchase the plan themselves pay their premiums directly. If the Tier 2 plan is acquired through an incentive or as part of a benefit package, a third party pays the premium.

Patients who do not have Tier 2 insurance coverage and receive a Tier 1 service are not charged (and do not get a bill). If patients receive a Tier 2 service and do not have a Tier 2 policy, they must pay out of pocket. Conditions covered by Tier 2 (and Tier 3) are unlikely to be urgent or life threatening. Consumers are able to decide if they want to pay for a particular therapy or service with the knowledge that their conditions may be uncomfortable but not a danger to their overall health.

Alternatively, consumers may want to comparison shop for the best price and quality for the Tier 2 or Tier 3 service they are contemplating, especially if they do not have coverage for it. Hospitals are required to post fees for all Tier 2 and Tier 3 procedures and services they offer, a price that would include all "hidden costs" except for physician fees. Physician fees are posted separately (and individually) so that consumers can compare prices for the hospitals and providers affiliated with that hospital.

Knowing the price of therapy and testing helps when comparison shopping for a Tier 2 or Tier 3 service. It may also drive down the costs of tests and procedures because providers, such as hospitals and doctors, must compete with one another. This competition not only helps to keep prices low, but it may press providers to offer better service and quality.

To truly understand how EMBRACE will feel to the average consumer, one needs to experience it firsthand. Because EMBRACE does not yet exist, an alternative universe must be created where both the current system and EMBRACE exist.

Next, you will read about two men who, to the casual observer, may appear to be identical twins but who in fact are the same person, separated only by time and reality. They have the same genetic composition, the same job, and the same wife and kids, and they live in the same house. However, Peter lives in our current reality, while Evan lives in a world where EMBRACE has been in effect for twenty years. I asked Peter and Evan to discuss their healthcare experiences in their respective worlds.

Can you please tell us a little about yourself?

Peter (current system): *I am a sixty-seven-year-old man, married for thirty-five years, with two children and one grandchild. I am* *self-employed as a consultant, a job I started when my company decided to "outsource" my position after a merger. My wife, Stephanie, is now sixty-four years old and was a schoolteacher until we had a family; she has been a stay-at-home mother ever since. Our son, David, is twenty-six years old and works as an engineer at a small start-up company, and our daughter, Sara, is twenty years old and starting her junior year of college.*

I had a heart attack five years ago and am now taking three medications. I also have high blood pressure and severe arthritis of the knees; the right is much worse than the left. My wife has diabetes and high blood pressure, both of which she controls with medication. Luckily, both of our children are healthy.

Evan (EMBRACE): *Ditto.*

Can you describe your health insurance experience?

Peter (current system): *Well, for the past two years, I have had Medicare, but up until I reached the age of sixty-five, I had at least four different types of insurance situations.*

For years, I worked for a large firm that offered health insurance coverage for all employees and their families. It covered most of our medical bills for visits to doctors' offices and hospitals. Of course, we did have a yearly deductible, and each outpatient visit did have a copay, but at first, these were not so bad. There were also a limited number of doctors and hospitals that we could go to without incurring a higher fee. But, for the most part, it was reasonable.

Unfortunately, as our firm began to have some financial issues, the deductible and copay amounts increased (and it did not matter why we were visiting the doctor). Then, when I had my heart attack, we discovered that the insurance did not cover some things (like cardiac rehabilitation services) that the doctor believed were important.

My heart attack was serious, and I had a protracted course in the hospital and underwent several procedures that not only saved my life but also helped my subsequent heart failure. It turns out I was lucky to have been discharged when I was. I found out that my health insurance plan had a limit for what it would pay in a year (and another limit for what it would pay for a specific condition) that I was not aware of. In fact, I discovered that my coworkers who had decided on that particular health plan were not aware of this limitation, either. The amount of money that I would have had to pay would most likely have sent us into bankruptcy.

A year after my heart attack, my company transferred me to another state, and I learned that I had to get a completely new insurance plan. This was difficult; because of my heart condition, the premiums were higher and my employer balked. The company was having financial difficulties, which they blamed on, among other things, the high cost of health insurance. It was soon obvious that they were ready to fire me, but I was able to get an early retirement package that included part of my pension.

After I lost my job, I had interim insurance called COBRA, but I had to pay the premium that my former employer used to pay. After a few months of unemployment, we could not afford COBRA and joined the ranks of the uninsured. We tried to apply to Medicaid, insurance for the poor, but our situation would not allow us to enroll at the time.

Luckily, we had only some minor health issues, so our out-of-pocket expenses were not catastrophic. But we did put off a number of routine visits to our doctors and always lived with the threat of a catastrophic illness wiping away all our life savings.

After a couple of years of being uninsured, we heard that our state (Connecticut), like some others, had set up a special insurance plan for people like us. It was called the Charter Oak plan and was a public/private offering that accepted people with preexisting conditions. (Obamacare had not yet taken effect.)

Like tens of thousands of others, we happily enrolled in what seemed to be a good policy. But we soon found out that, although most hospitals accepted the insurance for admissions, most doctors' offices did not. I had to travel across the state to see a cardiologist who accepted Charter Oak because there were none in my area who did.

On my sixty-fifth birthday, I enrolled in Medicare. I was overjoyed at first, but I soon learned it wasn't so simple. First, you have to decide which Medicare plan you want: basic Medicare or Medicare Advantage. With basic Medicare, I would have to pay 20 percent of outpatient office visits, but I could get another plan called Medigap to cover that. With Medicare Advantage, I had a 15 percent copay but could not get supplemental insurance like Medigap. In addition, I discovered that with basic Medicare I could see any doctor or go to any practice in the country, while with a Medicare Advantage plan I had to keep to the list of doctors the insurance company gave me.

I finally decided to get the basic Medicare and purchased Medigap to cover the "doughnut hole" in coverage. It was relatively easy to find a Medigap private insurance plan that was right for me. Unfortunately, even though I am now covered, my wife is not as she is still under age sixty-five.

Evan (EMBRACE): I have to say I haven't really thought about my healthcare coverage since EMBRACE was introduced twenty years ago. There is no formal enrollment into Tier 1 services; everyone is covered, and it automatically starts the first time you need it.

I was automatically added into EMBRACE at my first doctor's visit. It was a pretty simple process. I filled out a web-based form that asked for my social security number and a couple of other forms of identification; it took me no more than ten minutes to complete. Since my wife's first medical experience with EMBRACE was a hospital admission, her addition into the system was done then. My son was added when he visited his pediatrician, and my daughter was one of the first babies born after EMBRACE was implemented and was automatically added at the time of birth.

Once enrolled in Tier 1, every subsequent medical office visit and hospital admission required only a simple show of identification. The rest of my coverage information is linked to my online medical record.

When my company downsized, there was no change in my insurance coverage. When I had my heart attack, I knew that my Tier 1 insurance would never run out during my hospital stay. After I was discharged, my cardiac rehab service and all subsequent outpatient doctors' visits related to my heart condition were fully covered as well.

When my job required us to move, we did not have any changes in our health insurance (in fact, we hardly thought about it). Then, when I was laid off, my entire family had no change in coverage. There is no such thing as COBRA under EMBRACE because it is not needed.

Tier 2 coverage was a little more involved. But because it was optional and Tier 1 covered us for all serious or potentially serious conditions, we did not feel a need to buy Tier 2 coverage right away. I did not mind paying the occasional Tier 2 fee when I went to the doctor for my arthritis.

Once I had met certain goals that my doctor set for me, however, I was rewarded with free Tier 2 coverage. And, as long as my blood pressure and diabetes are controlled and I do not take up smoking again, my Tier 2 coverage will continue to be free.

My wife did not meet her goals, so she did not get free Tier 2 coverage. However, as we got older and saw that the price of Tier 2 insurance was quite reasonable, we decided to purchase a plan for her.

To purchase Tier 2 coverage, my wife went on the HealthMart website and was directed to a menu of offerings. This menu sounds similar to the one Peter described for Medigap. The plans had minimal criteria specific to each category, and every plan was fully portable, no matter what state we lived in.

Once we enrolled, our Tier 2 plan was fully integrated into the system. If we need office visits or procedures not covered by Tier 1, Tier 2 automatically kicks in (as long as the service is covered by the plan).

When I reached the age of sixty-five, nothing changed for me; my coverage remained and will continue to remain the same.

Please describe your outpatient experiences.

Peter (current system): My outpatient experiences changed depending on what insurance I had at the time, my employment status, and my age. When my company supplied our health insurance, we had a plan that allowed us to see any physician we wanted—often without the need for a referral from a primary care provider or approval from the insurance company.

But, over the years, both my employer and the insurance company wanted to save money. First, the deductible (a fixed amount of money I must pay before most, if not all, of the policy's benefits accrue) and copayments (parts of the medical bill not covered by insurance that must be paid by me) started to rise. Then, there were several limitations put on which doctor or healthcare provider I could see.

For example, if I wanted to make an office visit to the cardiologist who treated me in the hospital after my heart attack, I had to pay a premium; he was not one of the "preferred cardiologists" on the insurance company's panel. Initially, I went to one of the preferred doctors, but it was soon obvious that he did not know me as well as the cardiologist who had treated me. So I decided to pay the extra fee to see him.

The insurance company paid for a few sessions of cardiac rehabilitation. But the company refused to pay for a long-term exercise program, even though my doctor felt it was extremely important. I paid for a few sessions. But as financial pressures at home increased, I decided to discontinue the program, much to the dismay of my cardiologist.

When I was transferred to Connecticut, I could not keep the same policy, and the premiums on the new policies were higher with fewer benefits. In addition, the insurance company increased copays and deductibles, so my out-of-pocket costs increased significantly.

After I lost my job, I had to pay out of pocket for all of my doctors' visits and any tests they might order. Needless to say, I only went to the doctor when it was urgent and second-guessed the need for (and often refused) any tests they ordered.

As I mentioned before, we eagerly enrolled in our state's Charter Oak plan and paid reasonable premiums. Unfortunately, we soon discovered that none of our doctors accepted Charter Oak. In fact, we found that very few primary care doctors—and almost no specialists—accepted the insurance. I had to travel across the state to see one of the only cardiologists in the plan.

I learned that only a small number of doctors were in Charter Oak's limited plan because it paid them a fraction of what Medicare paid. So very few doctors and office-based practices accepted our insurance, and we made very few outpatient visits. However, Charter Oak assured us that they would provide coverage if we ever needed to be admitted to the hospital. We stayed on the plan until the state healthcare exchange opened under Obamacare in 2013.

Shopping for insurance under the new healthcare exchange was somewhat complicated. First, I had to declare my earnings for the past year and estimate my potential future earnings. This was difficult as I was still unemployed and working as a consultant. If I made less than a certain amount, I might be eligible for Medicaid, but if I made more than that amount, I had to enroll in one of the plans on the exchange. Unfortunately, I calculated that I made too much to qualify for Medicaid. But the good news was that I was eligible for a subsidy for one of the private insurance plans on the exchange.

The difficult part of shopping on the state exchange was finding a plan whose network included my doctor and then comparing the features and prices of the different plans I was considering. Each plan offers so many different features that I had to sort through them all before I finally found the one that fit my needs. For example, even though my daughter can be covered by my plan because she is under twenty-six years old, some types of HMO plans will only cover her for emergency visits because she is out of state and out of network.

Finally, on my sixty-fifth birthday, I eagerly applied for Medicare, but I soon found that it only covered 80 percent of my office-based doctor bills. Unless I purchased a supplemental plan, I had to pay the remaining 20 percent, even if it was for treatment of my heart disease or risk factors associated with it. The price of the supplemental insurance, called Medigap, was relatively low, so we went to the Medigap website and picked the one that best fit our needs.

Alternatively, I could have enrolled in what is called a Medicare Advantage plan. This offers additional services, such as eyeglass prescriptions, as well as a fairly low 15 percent deductible. But with these "privatized" plans, I could not buy a supplemental plan. In addition, because private insurance companies run Medicare Advantage, it limits the number of providers, much like regular private health insurance.

Unfortunately, because my wife is a couple of years younger than I am, she has to continue with the cheapest insurance we could find on the health exchange. Additionally, we are worried that when my wife does reach the age of sixty-five, our daughter will lose her coverage again, as Medicare does not cover other family members.

But I guess that wasn't the question you asked; was it? You asked about my outpatient experiences. As you can see, the insurance issues are a huge part of the overall experience when I go to the doctor. Every visit to a new doctor involves a lengthy ritual of filling out insurance forms and finding the right insurance card(s). There are questions about primary insurance and secondary insurance, as well as prescription plans. This was the case even after I enrolled in Medicare.

Although the paperwork is less extensive on subsequent visits, the insurance is constantly being updated and verified. At the end of the visit, I have to cover any copays. But, generally, the doctor submits the bill to the insurance company, which lets me know how much of my visit is covered.

When I do get the bill from the insurance company, it rarely covers everything, and I have to pay the remainder. This often leads to a period of negotiation with the insurer, where I often feel at a complete disadvantage. Frequently, I have spent hours on the telephone trying to resolve issues with the insurance company, which seems to thrive on such encounters. I am sure that much of this is just an intentional technique to discourage appeals.

Often, even my doctor visit is influenced by my insurance. When I needed cardiac rehabilitation after my heart attack, the doctor had to find out if it was covered. Once he determined that it was not, he had to spend extra time explaining to me how to safely perform exercises.

When my internist wanted to find me a rheumatologist for my arthritis, he discovered that the one he trusts the most was not in my insurance company's network. He then proceeded to look up a name in a pamphlet that the insurance company supplied him and chose a rheumatologist he did not know. Luckily, she was a decent doctor, but both my primary care doctor and I felt that these obstacles prevented me from receiving the best patient care.

Another problem we seem to have whenever we switch doctors, or go to a new hospital, is that it is difficult to have our medical records transferred. It seems that even if the doctors or hospitals have electronic records, there is no guarantee that the computers can "talk" to one another or that the records can be easily transferred. In addition, if we have had any testing—especially testing that involves images—the results often cannot be easily transferred from office to office or hospital to hospital. Consequently, we often need to have the test preformed again.

Evan (EMBRACE): *Wow! That's quite a story!*

Under EMBRACE, it is a lot simpler to get quality patient care. There is no policy to buy or select for the basic plan, and every provider who is qualified to practice accepts Tier 1 coverage; there are no "provider panels" that restrict who I can see.

When I had my heart attack, I had no problem getting a free follow-up appointment with the cardiologist who did my procedure. When I needed to see a specialty cardiologist, I found one at the Cleveland Clinic who was covered for all of my visits.

There are no deductibles or copayments with Tier 1 services. In addition, because EMBRACE is a nationwide plan and is not tied to any job, income, or military status, I have not had any interruption in the basic service since I first joined EMBRACE twenty years ago. When I did purchase Tier 2 coverage, it, too, was completely "portable"—and fairly inexpensive.

When I go to a new doctor, he or she can access all of my information on the secure EMBRACE electronic web record using my social security number. My medical records and test results are in the system—and available to my new doctor. The doctor enters the record of my visit and completes the UBF right away. If I have incurred any Tier 2 charges, I will be aware of this before I leave. If I have any Tier 2 or Tier 3 charges, I can either pay at the doctor's office or be billed. Of course, if I have Tier 2 insurance, the services are billed directly to the insurance company. If my visit with the new doctor falls entirely under Tier 1 services, I do not have to pay, and I do not get a bill.

Please describe your experiences with hospital care and procedures.

Peter (current system): *Again, much of my experience with hospital care and procedures depended on my insurance—or lack of it.*

I never had trouble getting treatment in an emergency, regardless of my insurance status. However, I knew that I would be billed for the visit. When I had insurance, the bill was only for what the insurance did not cover; when I did not have insurance, it was for the entire cost of the visit and treatment. And the price that the hospital charged when I did not have insurance was more than twice what it charged the insurance company for the same diagnosis! It seems that the insurance companies get a huge discount on what the hospital charges.

When the procedure or admission is elective, there is more bureaucracy involved. First, the doctor (or his or her office) must get a precertification, which means that the insurance company has to approve what the doctor ordered. My doctors all hate this process but have accepted it as a way of life. When I get to the hospital, they ask for my insurance card again, and I have to sign a form promising to pay whatever costs the insurance company will not. Even as I am getting ready for discharge, I have often found that the doctors order outpatient tests and prescribe medicines based on my insurance status.

When I get my bill (usually a few weeks after I am discharged), I find the information to be very complicated and confusing—and often, the bill includes charges from doctors I have never met.

If I go to the emergency room and am admitted to the hospital, Medicare pays for the whole visit. However, if I am put on a status called "observation," I receive the same level of care but have to pay 20 percent of the bill—even if I have a potentially life-threatening problem like chest pain or palpitations. The doctors give me the option of staying in the hospital under "observation" (and paying the bill) or signing a form that I am leaving against medical advice.

Evan (EMBRACE): With EMBRACE, almost all emergency hospital admissions are free of charge. I must provide my identity number or card so that my file can be accessed. But as long as my condition is determined to be Tier 1, which almost all emergency cases are, I never see a bill. Even when it is unclear whether I have a serious problem, if I am admitted for tests (similar to what Medicare calls "observation" status), the entire workup to rule out a life-threatening condition is free of charge.

The elective admissions or admissions for procedures are a little more involved. First, the doctor determines whether the admission is covered under Tier 1 with a quick inquiry via computer; this is done while I am in the office. If it is determined that the admission or procedure is covered under Tier 1, there is no charge. I am also covered if it is determined to be a Tier 2 procedure or admission and my Tier 2 insurance policy covers the services. If, however, the service falls at the Tier 2 level and I do not have insurance that covers it, my doctor can tell me what I will be charged—and I will know the price ahead of time.

The price that the doctor states includes both his or her services and what the hospital or clinic charges. I then have the option of accepting that price or shopping around for a better *one. The ability to know the price ahead of time is also true for Tier 3 services.*

Sometimes, as in the case of my arthritis, I have found that I prefer to keep my money rather than to have an operation; other times, an operation is worth the money.

It is important to understand that this applies only to non-Tier 1 services and conditions and services that will not put my health or life in danger. I have never had to make a financial decision about Tier 1 services—and I never will.

So ends this chapter on how EMBRACE might affect consumers/patients. Each person is unique and may have very different experiences in both the current system and under EMBRACE. However, it is quite likely that most consumers will notice a significant reduction in out-of-pocket costs and in the bureaucracy associated with medical insurance.

TABLE 2A. Comparison of EMBRACE, current, and single-payer systems' features for consumers

Consumer features	EMBRACE	Current system	Single-payer†
Universal coverage	Tier 1: yes	No	Yes
Access to doctors/hospitals	Unlimited	Limited by insurance coverage	Limited by insurance coverage and geography
Out-of-pocket fees to consumers	Tier 1: none Tier 2: annual fees, copayments, deductibles	Yes: annual fees, copayments, deductibles	Single payer: none Private: annual fees, other fees
Portability	Fully portable	Very limited (except original Medicare)	Fully portable
Possibility of personal bankruptcy	Low	High (1.7 million/year)[17]	Low
Personal paperwork	Low	High	Moderate
Ease of acquiring coverage	Tier 1: automatic Tier 2: easy via HealthMart	Medicare: moderate All others: difficult	Single payer: easy Private: moderate
Choice of provider (doctor/hospital/clinic)	Unlimited	Limited (depending on insurance)	Unlimited

Note: This table compares different features of EMBRACE to the current American health-care system and a proposed American single-payer system. One must keep in mind that because neither EMBRACE nor an American version of a single-payer system currently exists, some of the claims listed here are best estimations.

† Because one cannot predict which single-payer model might be adopted in the United States, the NHI proposal and/or the Canadian system is used for comparison.

---

10 "'Face the Nation' Transcripts, July 1, 2012: Speaker Boehner, Senators Schumer and Coburn, Governors Walker and O'Malley," http://www.cbsnews.com/news/face-the-nation-transcripts-july-1-2012-speaker-boehner-senators-schumer-and-coburn-governors-walker-and-omalley.
11 "White House Ready to Move on and Implement Health Care Law; McConnell: We Can Defeat Obamacare in November, Fox News, July 1, 2012, http://www.foxnews.com/on-air/fox-news-sunday/2012/07/02/white-house-ready-move-and-implement-health-care-law-mcconnell-we-can-defeat-obamacare-no?page=4#p//v/1715106182001.

12   Ajay Tandon et al., "Measuring Overall Health System Performance for 191 Countries," World Health Organization. http://www.who.int/healthinfo/paper30.pdf.

13   Karen Davis, Cathy Schoen, and Kristof Stremikis, "Mirror, Mirror on the Wall: How the Performance of the U.S. Health Care System Compares Internationally," (2010 Update). http://www.commonwealthfund.org/%7E/media/Files/Publications/Fund%20Report/2010/Jun/1400_Davis_Mirror_Mirror_on_the_wall_2010.pdf.

14   J. Hadley et al., "Covering the Uninsured in 2008: Current Costs, Sources of Payment, and Incremental Costs," *Health Affairs* 27, no. 5 (2008): 399.

15   G. Anderson, "From 'Soak the Rich' to 'Soak the Poor': Recent Trends in Hospital Pricing," *Health Affairs* 26, no. 4 (2007): 780–89.

16   David U. Himmelstein et al., "Medical Bankruptcy in the United States, 2007: Results of a National Study," *American Journal of Medicine* 122, no. 8 (2007): 741–46. http://www.pnhp.org/new_bankruptcy_study/Bankruptcy-2009.pdf.

17   Christina LaMontagne, "NerdWallet Health Finds Medical Bankruptcy Accounts for Majority of Personal Bankruptcies," *NerdWallet,* March 26, 2014, http://www.nerdwallet.com/blog/health/2014/03/26/medical-bankruptcy.

3

Healthcare Professionals

SUMMARY OF BENEFITS

- Place qualified healthcare professionals in charge of running the healthcare system.
- Allow doctors to maintain independence in decision-making.
- Allocate more time for clinical practice.
- Continue current practice settings (private office, HMO, hospital, etc.).
- Keep current coding in a fee-for-service system (no need to learn a new system).
- Provide instant credit for most services rendered.
- Enable easy and inexpensive integration of EMRs into practice.
- Eliminate or greatly reduce administrative overhead spent on obtaining preapprovals, appealing denials, and processing billing.
- Gain easy access to patients' medical records and testing.
- Integrate "Maintenance of Certification" requirements into clinical practice.

Given the recent attention focused on the ACA and other forms of "healthcare reform," it is easy to forget that the backbone of any successful healthcare system is the healthcare professional—especially the doctors and nurses who directly provide care. Unfortunately, most of what has been called healthcare reform comes from politicians and is directed toward health insurance reform (increasing coverage) and making healthcare delivery more efficient (less expensive). In addition, most of these reforms appear to be developed with the notion that the best way to transform the clinical practice of healthcare professionals is by altering their economic rewards and penalties in a way that forces them to adopt more efficient practices. Although some of these initiatives have reined in some of the escalating costs of healthcare, they have done little to make healthcare delivery better. Moreover, they have made the job of healthcare professionals significantly more difficult.

Healthcare professionals' lack of involvement in designing and running the American healthcare system is a tremendous missed opportunity for creating not only a better system in the way of outcomes but also a more efficient and patient-friendly system. Healthcare professionals have a unique point of view—one that comes from being at the "point of care"—or, as some might say, in the trenches. This perspective highlights the many flaws and bright spots that lawmakers and "public health experts" involved in healthcare reform might miss. Taken into account, this perspective might bring about more effective healthcare solutions.

For example, one area of office practice that healthcare economists and reformers have completely overlooked is the oppressive burden of insurance management. Although there are no formal studies on it (maybe because it has not been recognized as a problem), an informal polling of physicians in private practice reveals that most report the need to hire approximately one full-time employee just to handle patients' insurance. This employee, who often receives full benefits including health insurance, is paid out of the money the doctor collects from the insurance payments. If the doctor did not hire this person, he or she would have to take a significant amount of time away from treating patients to do this work, which would make him or her less efficient. One recent report estimated that the cost of processing insurance forms is fifty-eight dollars for every patient visit to a primary care physician.[18]

It is difficult to say how much of a physician's revenue goes to paying for this medically unnecessary expenditure. But it is likely that as much as 20 to 30 percent of the premiums that most consumers pay go to the overhead created by private insurance companies.

Despite the aid of these billers, a majority (70 percent) of office-based physicians report spending at least one full day a week on administrative work—and this number is increasing every year. This in part has led almost half (47 percent) to conclude that they will probably not be able to accept new patients—which in turn makes it harder for patients to find doctors, even if they have insurance.[19]

A related issue facing most healthcare professionals is what is commonly called an authorization or precertification. These are processes whereby doctors or nurse practitioners must obtain insurance company approval before ordering or performing a test or procedure. Officially, these steps are meant to ensure that the testing or procedure is deemed medically necessary. But it is very clear that the real reason is that the insurance companies are attempting to save as much money as possible. For practitioners, this is not only another hurdle in the process of providing care but also represents a level of oversight that is demeaning and unlikely to help patients.

The criteria that insurance companies use to determine the medical necessity of a test are based only partially on scientific evidence. Instead, these "appropriate-use criteria" are constructed using a complicated formula of cost and risk. Adding insult to injury for the treating doctor, non-physicians often deliver the approval or disapproval verdicts, with little understanding of or concern for the physician's judgment or the individual patient's benefit.

To make matters worse, each insurer may use different sets of criteria to determine which tests and procedures they will approve. Any mistake in this process may lead to a delay in service or even a denial of payment to the doctor. Still more distressing for the clinician is that payment for the same service may vary from one insurance company to another, making it difficult to make business decisions regarding hiring and capital investments.

Another major issue that has affected many office-based practices is the push to have EMRs replace paper charting. Theoretically, making all medical records available electronically allows quick access to clearly documented records of patient files. However, in reality, many issues have arisen because of this transition. First, the price of these systems is prohibitively expensive. A complete electronic record for a small practice of three or four providers can cost $10,000 or more *per provider*, an investment with little monetary return. It may be more efficient to bill through the medical record (if that feature exists). Yet there is no doubt that it takes doctors longer to complete an electronic record than a paper one, even after they become familiar with the system. This in turn wastes valuable physician time.

However, the most pernicious potential problem with the push to adopt universal EMRs is a computer's inability to communicate among records from different systems. Medical practices and hospitals depend on the ability to exchange patient information quickly and seamlessly, so the ability to access these records is essential. Because there is no standard "language" for medical records and other medical communication, information technology companies have little incentive to develop systems that communicate with systems made by other firms.

In addition, medical information firms could potentially become insolvent. This may not be a major problem if the software and hardware is compatible with other systems. But any incompatibility could lead to what can be called the Betamax syndrome.

Those who lived through the 1980s may remember two major videotape systems—VHS and Betamax—that competed with each other. Many experts believed that Betamax was the better system. But because of various business decisions, it ultimately lost out to the VHS system and was discontinued. Millions of people were left with Betamax tape players and tapes that were not only obsolete but also incompatible with the VHS system. This example illustrates that competition can lead to more robust innovation. But it is important to ensure that if the loser in the competition drops out, the consumer is not affected by the Betamax syndrome.

The investment in medical information systems by private practices and hospitals is substantial. Falling victim to the Betamax syndrome could not only adversely affect patient care, but it might also threaten the solvency of the practice itself.

In addition to the push by insurance companies to adopt electronic health records, physicians must contend with an arduous process of board certification and recertification. Like all professionals, doctors must keep an active license to practice in their fields—but hospitals and private practices have recently started to require that doctors also be board certified in their fields.

In the past, most physicians became board certified by completing a training program and then passing a certifying exam. Every ten years, doctors would have to pass a recertification exam for each of their specialties. Recently, the recertification process has become significantly more involved. In addition to maintaining a license and taking board recertification exams, doctors are now required to take several smaller tests every two years and perform many time-consuming "self-evaluation" projects related to their practices.

In addition to the significant expense of this process, doctors must devote a large amount of time to studying for and taking the exams, as well as performing the self-evaluation projects. This is time spent away from patient care.

EMBRACE'S SOLUTIONS

For the healthcare provider, EMBRACE preserves most of the current system's best features and drastically improves many of the most troublesome. It also helps healthcare providers deliver the best, scientifically validated therapy to their patients with a minimum of bureaucratic and financial burdens.

Central to this is the HIP (Healthcare Information Platform) and its provider interface, the UBF (Universal Billing Form). The HIP is a secure web-based platform available to every licensed healthcare provider in the country. When providers log into the HIP, they see a UBF. They enter basic identifying information about the patient, and the patient's medical chart becomes available immediately. Providers then use their own electronic medical charting program to record the patient visit.

Although the HIP is a common platform, each office, hospital, and nursing facility provides its own form of EMRs that comply with the HIP platform. Like the Apple operating system, application developers will be able to develop apps and hardware that seamlessly integrate with the HIP. These apps may include EMRs or software to view tests, such as echocardiograms or MRIs. And because they all share a common platform with required specifications, there is complete interoperability among systems and little risk of becoming a victim of the Betamax syndrome.

After the charting is completed by the healthcare provider, a copy goes to the provider's own server (as a patient file), and another copy is sent through the HIP to a national server. Concurrently, providers submit their bills using the existent Current Procedural Terminology codes (codes that determine types of service) and the International Classification of Diseases codes (codes that classify diseases). Once submitted, the HIP uses scientifically derived criteria to determine under which tier the service falls. If it is determined to be Tier 1, the provider is immediately credited (paid) for that service. If the service is determined to be Tier 2, the HIP searches to see if the patient has private insurance coverage. If the patient is covered, the HIP contacts the insurance company, and the provider is paid. If there is no insurance coverage for the service, the patient is billed for it.

In certain cases, it may be unclear to doctors and nurses whether the service they plan to give to the patient would be Tier 1 (where the patient would not have to pay), Tier 2, or Tier 3. In such cases, the provider simply adds a query to the UBF. This allows the provider the opportunity to discuss the options (and prices) with the patient, especially if the service is determined to fall under Tier 2 or Tier 3.

There are no precertifications or denials, and providers can do most of the billing themselves. Providers can appeal decisions, but these will be considered by the NMB in aggregate only; the appeals will not apply to the individual patient.

Another important clinical advantage of the HIP is that all testing results, no matter where the tests are performed, are available to all providers involved in a patient's care. This applies not only to laboratory tests of blood and other bodily fluids but also to pathology specimens and imaging studies. Imaging studies are provided, along with the physician's interpretation, and they also contain a link to access the image itself. In some cases, this access also includes the raw data originally collected by the imaging laboratory. In this way, the consulting doctor can reprocess the data if needed.

This ability to access the original testing data, rather than just someone's interpretation of the results, not only significantly improves patient care but also reduces the number of repeat tests required—and even reduces costs. In some instances (e.g., tests involving X-rays and nuclear agents), this reduces patients' exposure to harm, such as radiation.

EMBRACE simplifies the issue of board certification and maintenance of certification. The ABMS, which oversees certification, as well as the non-ABMS boards (such as those that certify doctors in nuclear cardiology or echocardiography), will either be taken over and reorganized by the NMB or disbanded. Either way, all oversight for the certification and maintenance of certification of healthcare professionals—including nurses and medical technicians—will be overseen by the NMB.

This change makes it possible to more fully integrate the process of maintaining certification into everyday practice. Providers can take online courses (offered through the HIP) specifically tailored to their specialties, eliminating the need to travel or take time off.

To better understand how EMBRACE might feel to the practitioner compared to our current system, let's meet two doctors. Dr. C is a primary care physician who has an office-based primary care practice in our current system. Dr. E, her identical twin, practices in the same office-based primary care practice in an alternate world where EMBRACE has been in place for twenty years. Although in reality it is impossible to know how EMBRACE will change practices over this period, it will significantly reduce the many administrative and financial burdens faced by office-based practices. These burdens are not always apparent, even to those who deal with them every day. I asked our two primary care physicians to describe what they do in their practice.

Can you please describe your daily office routine?

Dr. C (current system): *My office is fairly large. We have four physicians, two nurses, one receptionist, and three billers.*

In addition to greeting patients, making appointments, and answering the telephone, the receptionist spends much of her time updating insurance information and helping patients deal with insurance problems. The billers have several roles, which include submitting bills to the various insurance carriers and patients, getting approvals for testing and procedures, and appealing denials of payments. Because insurance stipulations and rules frequently change, these billers spend a lot of time simply keeping up with the changes.

Over the years, hiring these employees went from a luxury to a necessity, as the bureaucracy of the healthcare system increased and became more complicated. The only way our doctors and nurses could continue to have enough time for patient care was to hire these ancillary employees. Unfortunately, these employees do not help our patients, and they do not bring any revenue to our practice. We have to pay them from what insurance pays us to take care of patients; ironically, we also provide these employees with health insurance.

Because our staff is large, we have recently considered hiring an office manager to oversee the nonmedical staff.

On the clinical side, I have found that patients' insurance status often affects how I approach their treatment. Our practice occasionally accepts patients who don't have insurance; these patients pay out of pocket. We try to tailor their workups to avoid expensive testing or drugs, even when these are recommended by the science-based guidelines. But even when a patient does have insurance, I often have to check a list of approved tests and drugs before I order them. In addition, if I have to refer a patient to a specialist, I have to confirm that he or she is in the insurance company's approved panel. This is more prevalent with private insurance and Medicaid than with Medicare, but it complicates my workflow tremendously.

Around 2010, we had to convert our office charting to EMRs. This was originally done as an incentive, but after a few years, practices that had not adopted EMRs were fined. In addition, there was no subsidy for adopting EMRs and no guide for determining which systems were better rated. We chose one that cost almost $50,000 and took a considerable amount of time to install and learn how to use.

Although the ACA increased the number of insured patients we treat, the bureaucratic impediments to our practice have not gotten any better—and, in some respects, they have gotten worse. Although the copayments for some preventive care visits have been reduced or eliminated, they have often risen for other services.

In the past, we allowed forty-five minutes to see a new patient and twenty minutes for follow-up visits. These times have progressively gotten shorter (to less than thirty and ten, respectively). In addition, our reimbursements have decreased, and our nonpatient activities, such as paperwork for the insurance companies and Medicare, have increased.

Dr. E (EMBRACE): We also have four physicians, two nurses, and a receptionist, but we have no need for billers or an office manager.

When we see patients, we open their encounter forms on the computer and are able to download their entire charts instantly.

We have EMR software that we bought from a private vendor, just like an app you might buy on an Apple iPad. Because we bought the software through the HIP, it seamlessly interfaces with the platform. The software allows us to interface with all other EMRs on the system, regardless of whether they are generated by an office or hospital and no matter which vendor they use. Some practices even develop their own EMR applications so that they better fit the way they practice. Because all EMRs, labs, prescriptions, and bills must go through the HIP, they can all be completed with one online transaction.

We have wireless work pads that we take into every office and exam room. Everything we do with the patient is directly entered into a patient's chart via the work pad.

We do not have to ask for a patient's insurance status unless we are dealing with a Tier 2 or Tier 3 condition or treatment. If we choose a procedure that may be a non-Tier 1 service, a quick computer inquiry allows us to check to which tier it would be assigned. In addition, if it is Tier 2, we can determine whether the patient's insurance covers it. If it does not, we can quote a price for it that we set. Because the procedure or treatment under consideration is not lifesaving or preventive, the patient can always refuse and even go to another doctor for a better price.

Our practice has been able to maintain ample time for patient visits; we still allow at least forty minutes for an initial visit and twenty minutes for a follow-up. In addition, we have plentiful funds available to upgrade our facility.

Please tell us about how you get your medical education and maintain your board certification.

Dr. C (current system): *I am board certified in both internal medicine and pediatrics. In the past, this meant having to take recertification exams in each specialty every ten years. Because* of the time and expense required to prepare for each of these, I staggered them so that they were at least three years apart. Recently, the ABMS, the agency that oversees the certification process for both of my specialties, added several other requirements to maintain certification. Between the ten-year exams, there are five, two-year "modules" in which a physician must participate in some courses or other forms of learning and pass shorter exams. All of these activities take time out of my practice and, of course, cost a fair amount. In addition, each board requires that I conduct a self-assessment project on my practice, which again takes time away from my patients.

Dr. E (EMBRACE): When I finished my training, I was required to pass board exams in both internal medicine and pediatrics. Since then, I have maintained my certifications, mostly in my office, through the HIP.

There are many ways I can receive credit toward maintenance of my certification. On a daily basis, HIP tracks when I read online material pertaining to my patients' conditions. It also tracks when I read journal articles and, most important, when I review published guidelines. I can also take webinars for credit. Additionally, because the HIP is constantly tracking my patient activity, it can quickly furnish me with self-evaluation reports about my practice and even let me know how I compare with my peers.

Most of these activities are free of charge. I have found that I can easily integrate them into my practice without having to take time away from patients. Occasionally, I go to courses or meetings, especially when I need hands-on training in new procedures. These count toward my certification maintenance but must be entered separately.

So ends this chapter on how EMBRACE might affect healthcare professionals. Each provider is unique and may have different specialties and different practices. However, it is quite likely that most healthcare professionals will notice a significant reduction in the bureaucracy and expense associated with medical practice.

TABLE 3. Comparison of EMBRACE, current, and single-payer systems' features for healthcare professionals

Healthcare professional features	EMBRACE	Current system	Single payer†
Dealing with insurance verification and billing	Little to none	Very complicated	Single payer: moderate Private: unknown
Private practice	Encouraged	Trend toward hospital ownership and large groups	No change
Office bureaucracy	Little to none	Onerous	Single payer: moderate Private: unknown
Office overhead related to insurance	Little to none	As high as 20%	Little
EMRs	Easy to integrate	Difficult and expensive to integrate	Moderately easy
Cost of integrating EMRs	Low to moderate	Expensive	Moderate
Continuing medical education	Integrated into system	Expensive and time consuming	Not addressed

Note: One must keep in mind that because neither EMBRACE nor an American version of a single-payer system currently exists, some of the claims listed here are best estimations.

† Because one cannot predict which single-payer model might be adopted in the United States, the NHI proposal and/or the Canadian system is used for comparison.

---

18 Daniela Drake, "How Being a Doctor Became the Most Miserable Profession," *Daily Beast* Tech+Health, 4/14/2014, http://www.thedailybeast.com/articles/2014/04/14/how-being-a-doctor-became-the-most-miserable-profession.html.
19 CareCloud /QuantiaMD. "Second Annual Practice Profitability Index. Tracking the Operational and Financial Health of US Physician Practices," 2014, http://www.carecloud.com/practice-profitability-index-2014/.

4

Hospitals

- Maintain current models (community, not-for-profit, for-profit, religious-affiliation, specialty-hospital, veterans, etc.).
- Allow hospitals to predict insurance coverage and revenue.
- Significantly reduce administrative costs for billing and collections.
- Enable hospitals to have more control over EMR implementation and customization.
- Permit hospitals to easily acquire meaningful data about volume and quality.

The diversity of hospitals in the US healthcare system is fairly unique in the industrialized world. In 2012, there were more than fifty-seven hundred hospitals registered with the American Hospital Association in the United States, which includes federal hospitals (such as those run by the VA), nonfederal psychiatric hospitals, nonfederal long-term-care hospitals, prison-based hospitals, college infirmaries, and community hospitals. Community hospitals make up the largest group and can be nongovernment, not-for-profit, or for-profit, as well as institutions run by the state and local governments. Most community hospitals are "general" and admit a variety of patients, while others focus on specialties, such as cancer; obstetrics/gynecology; eye, ear, nose, and throat; rehabilitation; and orthopedics.[20]

Compared to hospital systems in other countries, those in the United States have the highest administrative costs, which account for about 25 percent—or more than $200 billion—of total hospital costs per year. The administrative costs seem to be correlated directly with the degree of penetration of "market-oriented payment" (private insurance rather than single payer) into the healthcare system. Countries that primarily use single-payer systems incur half of our system's costs.[21] This suggests that the reduction of US administrative costs would best be accomplished with a simpler and less market-oriented payment scheme, such as EMBRACE.

The incredible variety of hospital types in the United States has grown out of our uniquely complex healthcare system, which has both disadvantages and advantages.

The main disadvantages of the system are its redundancy and inefficiency. Hospitals duplicate services; alternatively, because of budgetary considerations, some services are underrepresented compared with need. Further, more lucrative services may be overrepresented. This means that there may be longer waits for some services (or even no service) for underrepresented services, while the overrepresented services might cause wasted resources and even a dilution of experience for doctors and other medical personnel. How would you like to have your heart surgery performed by a surgeon who only does five a year?

Because some hospitals, such as those that treat veterans or those belonging to a particular HMO, accept different insurance than do others, patients are limited to participating hospitals for their regular care. This significantly limits the choice and even mobility of the patient/consumer, as there may be only a limited number of participating hospitals.

A rather disturbing secret is that most American hospitals tailor medical care based on a patient's insurance status. Although this might seem unfair and maybe even discriminatory, for the most part, it is really done for the patient's benefit. If patients lack insurance or have inadequate insurance, they may be unable to afford their medications and outpatient testing. Consequently, the care team, which often is different for these patients than for "private" patients, might elect to do testing and treatments in the hospital that would more appropriately be done in an outpatient capacity. Further, doctors might prescribe cheaper—and possibly less effective—medications on discharge.

Because the uninsured pose significant financial pressures, hospitals in poorer areas have more limited funds and therefore have a harder time providing the best services to their patients, even those who have insurance. This discrepancy is compounded by the fact that these hospitals tend to be in regions with sicker populations that rely more than others do on hospital-based care.

In addition, the way that hospitals are paid by Medicaid and Medicare is variable, unpredictable, and mired in politics. This makes it all the more difficult for hospitals to make business decisions and devise future financial plans.

There are, however, some good aspects of the US hospital system, such as serving their communities. In addition, competition with other facilities often results in better-quality facilities and facility improvements.

The specialized aspect of the US hospital system is not unique. Most industrialized countries have a similar stratified system, from the local "general" or community hospital to the large tertiary teaching hospitals, such as the Mayo Clinic, that may take referrals from all over the country (and even the world). What makes the US system different is that the government runs only a few hospitals (about 20 percent). More than 90 percent of hospitals in European countries with some form of single-payer systems, such as Sweden and the United Kingdom, are considered to be government run.[22]

Although the merits of government-run hospitals are debatable, in the United States there is clearly a public preference for non-government-run hospitals. Much of this is due to the public perception that nongovernment hospitals provide better service and, maybe, better care. Certainly, the 2014 scandals involving the VA hospital system, where dangerously long patient wait times for treatment were allegedly covered up, serve to further that perception. Another common belief is that competition for patients among nongovernment hospitals not only improves service but may also improve the breadth and quality of care.

EMBRACE eliminates or greatly reduces most of the current system's disadvantages while maintaining the advantages. There is no difference in insurance status among patients for most hospital-based treatments, because most nonelective admissions tend to be Tier 1. Consequently, under EMBRACE, the bipartite system of insured/uninsured patients is a thing of the past. This not only improves patient care, but it also reduces hospital and healthcare system costs as a whole. There is significantly less need for specialists to treat the uninsured and underinsured. Additionally, because the rules for care under EMBRACE are the same for each patient, there is a greatly reduced need for social workers and medical billers.

Under EMBRACE, hospitals are allowed to create their own business plans. Each hospital decides on the price of its Tier 2 services and makes these prices available to the public; these are the prices charged to patients who do not have Tier 2 insurance. In addition, as in the current system, each hospital can negotiate with insurance companies for Tier 2 "contracted" rates, which will not need to be made public.

Tier 1 reimbursement rates are determined by the NMB on an individual basis, based on the region and its disease prevalence. These rates are reviewed and updated periodically through a process that involves both the hospital and the NMB's local representatives. Reimbursement includes outpatient preventive programs initiated and run by the hospital, as well as medical education for trainees, such as residents and nursing students.

TABLE 4. Comparison of EMBRACE, current, and single-payer systems' features for hospitals

Hospital features	EMBRACE	Current system	Single payer†
Fiscal independence	Strong	Strong	Weak
Ease of billing	Automatic	Very difficult	Single payer: easy Private: moderate
For-profit potential	Moderate	Strong	Very weak to none
Specialization potential	Strong	Strong	Weak
EMR integration	Easy	Difficult	Unknown
Fee transparency	High Tier 1: prices set by NMB Tier 2: prices set by hospital and posted publicly	Low Often different depending on insurance	Moderate to high Negotiated with central payer (Unknown for private insurance)
Hospital administrative costs	Moderate	High	Moderate

Note: One must keep in mind that because neither EMBRACE nor an American version of a single-payer system currently exists, some of the claims listed here are best estimations.

† Because one cannot predict which single-payer model might be adopted in the United States, the NHI proposal and/or the Canadian system is used for comparison.

20 Health Forum LLC, "Fast Facts on US Hospitals," from the 2014 AHA Annual Survey, American Hospital Association. http://www.aha.org/research/rc/stat-studies/fast-facts.shtml.
21 D. U. Himmelstein et al., "A Comparison of Hospital Administrative Costs in Eight Nations: U.S. Costs Exceed All Others by Far," *Health Affairs* 33, no. 9 (2014): 1586–94.
22 Fanny Chevalier Dexia and Judith Lévitan, under the supervision of Dominique Hoorens. "Hospitals in the 27 Member States of the European Union," Dexia Editions, January 2009, http://www.hope.be/05eventsandpublications/docpublications/79_hospitals_in_eu/79-hospitals-in-the-eu-2009.pdf.

5

Businesses

SUMMARY OF BENEFITS

- Free all businesses from the requirement to provide health insurance of any type.
- Automatically cover all employees for basic health insurance.
- Eliminate the need to negotiate health insurance contracts or manage plans.
- Dramatically reduce healthcare and benefit administration costs and efforts.
- Lower cost to cover health insurance for employees.
  - No requirements to provide health insurance to employees.
  - Employer taxes are determined by the number of employees and their salaries.
  - FICA-like taxes for employees remain the same.
- Offer tax breaks to businesses that promote a "healthy workplace" and prevention programs.
- Allow businesses to offer inexpensive, additional (Tier 2) insurance as an optional benefit.
  - Attract new hires.
  - Increase retention.
  - Provide disability supplements.
- Reduce the pressure on businesses to constantly improve plans.
  - Possibly simplify collective bargaining over health insurance.

- Eliminate retiree medical liabilities for firms with large retiree populations.
  - Possibly improve corporate balance sheets.

Although EMBRACE is designed primarily to improve the nation's healthcare system, its effect on business will be no less dramatic. Historically, health insurance was a benefit offered by businesses to employees. But it soon became an expected part of an employee's benefit package. Now, under ACA, employer-provided health insurance is mandated for businesses with more than fifty employees.

For many companies, health insurance is one of the biggest "benefit expenditures," representing an average of 7.6 percent of take-home salary in 2015 for private industry jobs, 8.3 percent for civilian jobs, and 11.6 percent for state and local government jobs.[23] This expense is not only a financial burden for businesses but can also be a distraction; businesses regularly have to negotiate with insurance companies on the terms of these plans.

Under the ACA, there has been little improvement for companies with more than fifty employees. In fact, as the minimal standards for insurance policies increase, it is likely that employer costs will also increase. Either way, the ultimate effect is that employer-based insurance will become codified into the private sector for large corporations.

For companies with fewer than fifty employees, there is likely to be a push to discontinue employer-based insurance, requiring employees to go to the health exchanges for coverage. Although this might be a good financial move for these small companies, it might ultimately hamper their growth, as they would need to invest a large amount of money when they transition from forty-nine to fifty or more employees.

The fact that much of the insurance purchased through employers in the current system is not portable also poses a burden to both employers and employees. Employees must change insurance providers every time they change a job, often having to spend hours enrolling in the policy offered by the new employer or a new policy through the health exchange.

Employers must inform each new hire about the benefits of the plan(s) they provide as well as help the new employee enroll.

Under EMBRACE, there is no requirement for employers to provide health insurance. Tier 1 already covers every employee for life, and there is never a need to reenroll. A payroll tax directly proportional to salary is levied on every employee. Other than that, there is no financial obligation to businesses.

Employers can offer Tier 2 coverage as a benefit if they choose. They can buy these policies through the HealthMart. Alternatively, they can negotiate directly with an insurance carrier for Tier 2 plans, as long as these conform to the approved minimum requirements for Tier 2 policies. Employers may also want to purchase Tier 2 disability insurance that would cover injuries not covered under Tier 1, such as back injuries.

Because all Tier 1 coverage is identical and requires no enrollment, there is no need to administer it. There is also no need to spend time and money on negotiating health insurance contracts or managed-care plans. If the employer wants to offer Tier 2 insurance, employees can easily—and directly—obtain it on the HealthMart.

Employers who invest in "healthy workplace" and other prevention programs for their employees may be eligible for a break on their healthcare taxes. When well designed, these money-saving programs may also reduce the number of employee absences and thereby increase productivity.

Likely the biggest savings to businesses, especially large ones, will involve retirees. Although not all businesses offer retirement health plans, almost half of the large corporations still do. In the current system (as of 2010), early retirees typically cost former employers $7,596 per year (compared with $5,184 for an active employee). Mainly because it is a supplement to Medicare, the cost of providing insurance to retirees sixty-five years of age or older is about $3,840 per year for an individual and $7,848 for an individual and a spouse.[24]

Because Tier 1 coverage under EMBRACE does not depend on employment or age, retirees are covered in the same way as they are when employed. The only cost to the employer is the healthcare tax on the pension the employee may receive, as it is considered a salary. This cost should be significantly lower than in the current system.

Employer-provided Tier 2 coverage is not required after retirement—but, if chosen, it should also be significantly less expensive than in the current system.

The benefits of EMBRACE to businesses go beyond financial savings. Because all employees receive identical Tier 1 coverage, there is a feeling of commonality. In addition, Tier 1 benefits reduce the pressure on employers to constantly improve their health plans and could simplify collective bargaining over health insurance. It is clear that many recent disputes between employers and labor unions have revolved around health insurance coverage.

If a system like EMBRACE had been in place several years ago, several large corporate bankruptcies, including General Motors, would likely have been avoided; the retiree medical costs provided through its collective bargaining process was crippling to its overall balance sheet.

Under EMBRACE, disability insurance for items not covered under Tier 1 is included under Tier 2. The HealthMart offers several disability insurance plans that either the employee or the employer can purchase. This means that those businesses that want to offer these bonuses can purchase and maintain the plan relatively simply. Those who are employed in a business that does not offer disability insurance, or those who are self-employed, can purchase a plan relatively easily and inexpensively.

TABLE 5. Comparison of EMBRACE, current, and single-payer systems' features for businesses

Business features	EMBRACE	Current system	Single payer†
Employer-mandated Coverage	None	For > 50 employees	None
Cost to businesses to manage health insurance	Tier 1: none Tier 2: very low to none	High	Low
Pension costs for health insurance	Low	High	Low

Note: One must keep in mind that because neither EMBRACE nor an American version of a single-payer system currently exists, some of the claims listed here are best estimations.

† Because one cannot predict which single-payer model might be adopted in the United States, the NHI proposal and/or the Canadian system is used for comparison.

---

23 US Bureau of Labor Statistics, "News Release: Employer Costs for Employee Compensation—December 2015." http://www.bls.gov/news.release/pdf/ecec.pdf.
24 Arlen Group, "Post-Retirement Health Insurance." http://www.arlengroup.com/facts/fact_postretire.pdf.

6

Government

SUMMARY OF BENEFITS

- Provide a patient/consumer-friendly system with universal coverage.
- Check or even reduce public expenditures on healthcare.
- Eliminate Medicare and Medicaid.
- Abolish the US Department of Health and Human Services and its healthcare-related subsidiary departments.
- Allow Congress to control the budget but not to develop and implement healthcare policy.
  - One annual budget for all healthcare expenditures.
  - Less time needed by Congress to deal with healthcare-related issues.
- Eliminate the need for states to subsidize healthcare coverage (i.e., Medicaid).
- Stop the impending bankruptcy of the Medicare Trust Fund.
- Free businesses from the need to provide healthcare insurance (economic benefit).
- Enable full participation of for-profit health insurance companies.
- Allow some "free-market" features without compromising the patient's health or affecting the publicly funded system.

I n a perfect world, it would be reasonable to say that government should have no part in delivering healthcare to its citizens. After all, what kind of medical training does the average lawmaker have, and how much does he or she understand about public health and prevention issues? However, because healthcare delivery is a commercial service, and all commerce is subject to laws and regulations, it is difficult to find any western society where government is not involved in healthcare to some degree.

In the United States, there are many elements of government involvement in healthcare administration. The most influential government agency is the US Department of Health and Human Services (HHS), a cabinet-level department that oversees many other agencies, such as the CMS, the CDC, and the NIH. This, in fact, makes healthcare a part of the government as well as a political target.

In addition, because Medicare, health programs run by the VA, and some parts of Medicaid are federally regulated, Congress has a constitutional role in financing these programs. This role should be a simple matter, but it has become a major political issue that has often threatened arbitrary cuts to funding for various programs, including Medicare and Medicaid.

Under EMBRACE, the establishment of an independent healthcare board and abolishment of the HHS should reduce a great deal of the politicization of healthcare. Like the Federal Reserve, a nongovernmental group that oversees much of the nation's money supply, the NMB under EMBRACE will be a mostly independent agency. As with the Federal Reserve, the NMB chair would be appointed every ten years—or a different term, such as five years—by the president and approved by Congress. Congress continues to control financing with one annual budget for the entire healthcare system.

This sum may seem much larger than the individual bills that finance different parts of the system. In the end, however, having one budget makes it easier to track costs and may actually reduce much of the redundancy in the current funding system.

As each annual funding bill is advanced, many robust discussions are likely to take place in Congress. However, there will be much less potential for earmarking and politicization of the various elements of these annual bills. More attention can be directed to the fiscal elements of the funding, which in turn will allow Congress to better control what it spends on healthcare. In addition, because there will be only one bill dealing with healthcare financing, there will be more time to spend on other congressional business.

Another significant advantage of EMBRACE is that it eliminates the threat of Medicare's impending bankruptcy. Briefly, this projected bankruptcy is because of the growing number of people covered by Medicare. As the baby boomers reach the age of sixty-five and their life expectancy increases, proportionally fewer people contribute to the Medicare Trust Fund. Under EMBRACE, coverage for the more limited range of Tier 1 services applies to the entire population and does not depend on a trust fund mechanism. Tiers 2 and 3 will be paid either out of pocket or through commercial insurance.

There are also many potential economic benefits under EMBRACE. Currently, employer-provided health insurance has been all but codified into our healthcare system. Even though it does not require businesses with fewer than fifty employees to provide health insurance, the ACA does require that larger companies offer these plans. In effect, this might limit the growth of successful start-ups as they reach that threshold size. In addition, the cost of acquiring and maintaining these plans often requires a significant amount of capital and personnel.

The universal portability of all elements of EMBRACE also provides a significant economic advantage over the current system. No longer will consumers need to reapply for insurance every time they move to another state or change jobs. With Tier 1 services, there is no need to enroll; every US citizen or green card holder is part of the program. This means that the expense and effort needed to determine eligibility, as well as the need for subsidy, as is the case with the current system, is eliminated.

Any plan offered through Tier 2 will be valid in every state. Although the price might vary according to the particular plan, consumers can be certain that the Tier 2 plan coverage they buy in one state will not change if they move out of state.

With the significant reduction in administrative costs for hospitals and office-based practices, there is a potential for huge savings with a system like EMBRACE. A recent study showed that if an EMBRACE-like system that reduced the administrative costs of health insurance were in place in the United States, it could potentially save about $150 billion a year.[25] These savings would come without limitations of service or a reduction in the quality of healthcare.

It is likely there will be a similar savings in administrative costs for office-based practices. Additionally, as there is an increased emphasis on shifting nonemergent care to outpatient settings, these savings will likely become more important.

At the state level, several features of EMBRACE should significantly reduce the financial burden on government. With the elimination of Medicaid, there is no need to finance part of the program's cost. Currently, Medicaid financing is split between the federally run CMS and each state. Some states supplement this funding robustly, while others fund only the minimum required by law. Either way, this feature should represent substantial savings.

Another major cost for state governments—and the federal government—is the cost of health insurance coverage for government workers. EMBRACE virtually eliminates this cost. The only exception might be if a state decides to offer Tier 2 coverage to its employees, but this will be up to the individual states and much less expensive.

In addition, because of the elimination of most uninsured patients and the overhead associated with billing, the financial situation of hospitals should improve. This in turn will reduce the political and financial pressures on state governments to provide assistance to hospitals in the state. This might be particularly valuable in states and cities like New York that have large publicly funded hospitals that currently treat many uninsured or underinsured patients.

Another advantage of EMBRACE is that there will be no need for state healthcare exchanges, as is now the case under the ACA. This should eradicate the political and financial elements associated with maintaining state exchanges or deferring to a federally run program.

Finally, one should not discount the financial and even political effects of having an efficient, streamlined, and nongovernmental healthcare system that reduces redundancy and emphasizes prevention and proven therapy. Despite some recent successes in reining in healthcare costs, the American healthcare system is still by far the most expensive system, per capita, in the industrialized world. Yet it ranks in the bottom third in measurable outcomes, such as maternal and infant death rates and overall life expectancy.

Most of the countries in which expenses are lower and outcomes are better have a single-payer system. This term implies that there is a single agency that oversees a country's entire healthcare system (and at the same time has no, or a very limited, role in private health insurance). This oversight of the entire healthcare system successfully allows for reduced costs and better outcomes.

A single-payer system would reduce the duplication of services, such as having a VA system that provides services similar to those covered by other hospitals and clinics. This duplication, which is a prominent feature of the American healthcare system, not only increases expenses but also causes such problems as limitation of access.

Recently, the Veterans Choice Program exemplified the limitation of access and increased cost. This program allows veterans in rural areas who live more than forty miles from a VA facility to use alternative (non-VA) medical facilities. The law was introduced because of the limited number of VA hospitals and clinics, forcing many eligible veterans to travel long distances to receive care. In response to complaints about the designated distance required to qualify for the benefit, Congress revised the law: just the change in defining the distance from "as the crow flies" to "driving distance" doubled the number of qualifying veterans. This change also doubled the cost to taxpayers, as the VA now had to pay for a duplicate service!

Another advantage of the single-payer system is that it makes it easier to coordinate public health policies and even to track epidemics and health trends.

At the same time, there are some significant limitations that may be encountered if the United States were to adopt a single-payer system. The most important downside is that it would likely increase taxes significantly. These increases are due to the need to fund services and treatments for about 60 percent of the population under the age of sixty-five who are now funded by private insurance. This, of course, is a very difficult thing to propose to the public, especially in the current political environment.

EMBRACE offers the best of both the current US system and a possible single-payer system but with fewer of the disadvantages of either. Because the entire US healthcare system will be organized under it, the NMB will have the same system oversight that characterizes single-payer systems. With the consequent elimination of most duplicated services, EMBRACE will facilitate and even increase access to medical services compared to the current system. Additionally, because private insurance will pay for a large portion of the healthcare spending (the exact figure is difficult to currently assess, but it will likely account for about 40 percent to 50 percent of national health expenditures), EMBRACE should require significantly lower public financing than single-payer systems.

In addition, under EMBRACE, the public receives basic (Tier 1) health insurance coverage that does not require annual fees, deductibles, co-pays, or even paperwork. The lifetime coverage is fully portable from state to state and from job to job and never requires enrollment—an unpopular feature of the ACA. Optional private insurance (Tier 2) is affordable, understandable, and, like Tier 1 insurance, fully portable.

Further, once the EMBRACE-inspired system is implemented, healthcare will cease to be a hot-button issue and a distraction for lawmakers.

It will allow governments to govern and healthcare professionals to treat, and it will bring our country's healthcare system into the twenty-first century.

However, let's be honest. For most lawmakers, the most important issue is if EMBRACE will save the US taxpayer money, and, if so, how. The answer is yes, and the following chapter summary explains how.

- EMBRACE will eliminate redundant funding by
  - integrating all federal healthcare agencies under the NMB, resulting in less duplication of services;
  - not requiring the VA system to have separate funding;
  - eliminating Medicare and Medicaid;
  - doing away with the need to supplement insurance payments for low-wage earners; and
  - making spending more transparent and manageable through one annual healthcare funding bill.
- EMBRACE will abolish state spending on Medicaid.
- EMBRACE will significantly reduce costs to federal, state, and local governments for health insurance coverage of government employees.
- EMBRACE will appreciably lower the government cost of implementing EMRs.
- EMBRACE will substantially reduce the financial burden on businesses and improve their international competiveness.
  - All employees will have health insurance.
  - Health insurance administrators will no longer be needed.
  - The workforce will become more mobile.
- EMBRACE will provide a very effective mechanism to implement preventive measures, which in turn will reduce the need to spend more on treating preventable conditions.

TABLE 6. Comparison of EMBRACE, current, and single-payer systems' features for government

Government features	EMBRACE	Current system	Single payer†
Funding	Simple: one annual bill for entire system	Extremely complex	Moderate (like funding for Medicare)
Direct federal system oversight	None	Moderate	High
Taxpayer costs	Moderate	Moderate	High
State costs	None	High	Depends on model
Universal coverage	Yes	No	Yes

Note: One must keep in mind that because neither EMBRACE nor an American version of a single-payer system currently exists, some of the claims listed here are best estimations.

† Because one cannot predict which single-payer model might be adopted in the United States, the NHI proposal and/or the Canadian system is used for comparison.

---

25 D. U. Himmelstein et al., "A Comparison of Hospital Administrative Costs in Eight Nations: U.S. Costs Exceed All Others by Far," *Health Affairs* 33, no. 9 (2014): 1586–94.

7

Private Insurance Companies

SUMMARY OF BENEFITS

- Substantially reduce financial risk for private (Tier 2) insurance providers, because the insurer will not be liable for Tier 1 payments.
- Allow risk profiling (e.g., preexisting conditions) and denial of coverage by private (Tier 2) insurance providers.
- Enable free-market pricing in the private (Tier 2) insurance market.
- Separate public insurance from private plans to avoid competition.

The role of private insurance (i.e., insurance not overseen by a government agency) in the US healthcare system is incredibly varied and unique as compared with practically any other system in the world. Developed in the early twentieth century as a workplace benefit advocated by labor unions, private insurance predates Medicare and Medicaid and was created with little help from physician groups such as the American Medical Association or from hospital groups.[26] Since that time, employer-funded—or at least employer-supported—health insurance has been one of the major sources of private plans in the country and remains so under the ACA, which has all but codified its presence.

With some exceptions, the firms that manage health insurance coverage are for-profit corporations, and most are publicly traded, which means that they are under considerable pressure to maximize profits. It has been argued that the for-profit nature of these companies might present a conflict of interest when it comes to what is best for a patient (or client), as their primary objective is to increase shareholder returns. This, some suggest, might lead insurance providers to color their coverage or payment decisions to increase profits, even to the potential detriment of their clients and healthcare providers (doctors, hospitals, etc.).

Denial of coverage is an example of how insurance companies weed out high-risk patients (i.e., clients who are likely to cost them money). One blatant example (before the ACA effectively disallowed it) was to block coverage for preexisting conditions. But there are still subtle ways to eliminate "high-risk" clients. One (possibly apocryphal) story tells of an insurance company that, when first rolling out its new Medicare Advantage (privatized Medicare) plan, held information sessions and enrollment on the second floor of a building that had no working elevator or escalator. This meant that potential clients who had a disability or were medically infirm could not make it up the stairs and would therefore be less likely to enroll.

Another method by which private insurance companies make a profit is by throwing roadblocks. One of the most widespread practices is requiring permission to perform a test or therapy. This practice, called preapproval or precertification, is one of the most irritating aspects of the current US medical system—both for providers and for clients—and it is also likely one of the most costly to our healthcare system.

However, even with all of these issues, there is still a major advantage in having a for-profit health insurance industry in the United States. As of 2014, private insurance contributed 33 percent of the estimated $3.0 trillion the US spends on healthcare.[27] This, of course, is money that does not have to be paid by public insurance or taxes.

In addition, there is a long tradition in this country's economic system and capitalistic traditions of involving private enterprise in the healthcare system. It is inconceivable that a healthcare system that did not include a major role for private insurance would have any chance of being accepted—either politically or economically.

Under EMBRACE, representatives from each insurance provider participate in the private insurance section of the NMB. Along with the rest of the board, this group establishes the menu of plans offered under Tier 2. The menu is loosely based on the Medigap menu that has been in use since the 1990s. (See chapter 2.)

Like the Medigap menu, there are several different Tier 2 plan options from which to choose. The options are listed side by side and indicate the minimum coverage benefits that the particular plan must include. Once consumers choose a plan, another menu (opened by a mouse click) appears that lists the insurance companies offering that plan. Because the first menu only lists the minimal coverage benefits, the second menu lists any additional benefits that the insurance company is offering with the plan for the price indicated. The price quote will include all copays and deductibles, as well as any yearly and lifetime limits on what the insurance company will pay.

Insurance companies are not required to participate in each plan option under EMBRACE. But if they do offer a particular plan, it must adhere to the minimal requirements in that category and be available in all states. (The NMB might possibly allow for a small variation in price quotes depending on the state.)

There are several potential benefits for insurance companies. One of the most significant is the reduced "risk" of having to pay out large sums of money to cover the most expensive treatments, as these are often covered by Tier 1. EMBRACE offers insurance providers a large potential clientele with a relatively low-risk profile. Because every US citizen is a member of EMBRACE, insurance companies have the entire population as potential clientele. Because every citizen will have Tier 1 coverage, the entire population is relatively low risk. Private insurance companies will not have to pay for the treatment of heart attacks, cancers, pregnancies, high blood pressure, diabetes, and other conditions. The potential liability is quite small and potential profits more secure.

Because preauthorization and other administrative processes are either eliminated or carried out by the UBF system, another benefit will be a significant savings in administrative costs (estimated at between 10 and 20 percent). In addition, as with automobile insurance, there may be a way to allow the insurance company to increase its premiums to individuals according to the number of claims and their payout amounts. This will not only limit "frivolous" Tier 2 claims by the insured, but it will also encourage the consumer to shop around for the best price for a particular therapy or service.

In addition, it is likely that the NMB will allow insurance companies to charge copays, have deductibles, and limit the total payments made for various Tier 2 conditions, the latter of which is not allowed under the ACA. Tier 2 coverage in EMBRACE may also allow the insurance carrier to exclude consumers who have preexisting (Tier 2 and possibly even Tier 1) conditions, something the ACA does not allow.

It is very likely that the profit potential for private insurers under EMBRACE is as good as, if not better than, the current system, and it is significantly better than a single-payer system would allow. (The single-payer NHI proposal would completely eliminate private insurance—at least officially.) For starters, Tier 1 generally includes what many insurers consider "risky" conditions. This means that the potential for huge payouts for these conditions will be eliminated. Most of the conditions assigned to Tier 2 are generally of limited expense—and mostly elective. This in turn means that patients/consumers have more time to assess whether they need the therapy or procedure and even to shop around for a better price or an alternative therapy, possibly with the aid of the insurer.

Like the current system (and unlike the single-payer system), health insurance companies under EMBRACE are allowed to be publicly traded but can also be not-for-profit and government agencies (e.g., the VA). This, of course, is at the discretion of the NMB.

TABLE 7. Comparison of EMBRACE, current, and single-payer systems' features for private insurance

Private insurance features	EMBRACE	Current system	Single payer†
Defined role in system	Yes	Yes	No
Affordability	Very affordable	Very expensive	Moderate expense
Ease of enrollment	Very easy	Difficult	Unknown*
Ease of comparison between plans	Very easy	Extremely difficult	Unknown*
Portability	Fully portable	Limited by job, state	Limited by state

Note: One must keep in mind that because neither EMBRACE nor an American version of single-payer system currently exists, some of the claims listed here are best estimations.

† Because one cannot predict which single-payer model might be adopted in the United States, the NHI proposal and/or the Canadian system is used for comparison.

*Almost all single-payer systems in free-market countries have some form of private insurance, which has developed separately from the original single-payer system. There are varying degrees of oversight for these plans. The independent growth of private insurance is likely to occur in the United States as well if a single-payer model is adopted. If such a system is actually adopted, it is very difficult to know how it will develop.

---

26   Peter A. Corning, "Chapter 1: The First Round—1912 to 1920," in *The Evolution of Medicare: From Idea to Law* (Washington, DC: Office of Research and Statistics, Social Security Administration, (1969), https://www.ssa.gov/history/corningchap1.html.
27 "National Health Expenditures 2012 Highlights," CMS.gov, http://www.cms.gov/Research-Statistics-Data-and-Systems/Statistics-Trends-and-Reports/NationalHealthExpendData/downloads/highlights.pdf.

8

Public Health

- Construct a healthcare system designed to take advantage of twenty-first century technology and innovation.
- Provide truly universal health insurance coverage.
- Feature an independent (nongovernmental) NMB that will
  - be guided by a "National Healthcare Mission" statement,
  - provide representation from all aspects of the health system,
  - integrate healthcare research with healthcare delivery,
  - provide an efficient mechanism for adopting guidelines for clinical practice, and
  - be able to commission studies specifically for guideline development.
- Encourage a greater focus on prevention.
- Include an automatic HIP that allows real-time detection of epidemics and other health concerns.
- Allow for universal registries with little effort or expense.
- Develop a mechanism to perform Phase IV studies on all medications and devices.
- Enable immediate identification of outbreaks and epidemics.

When it comes to public health in the United States, we are not doing so well. For years, we have been spending twice as much on healthcare per capita as most other industrialized countries, yet public health outcomes, such as life expectancy or infant and maternal death rates, are in the lower third.[28] The reasons for these grim statistics are complex and subject to considerable debate, but the facts emphasize the need for a sea change in the American healthcare system.

Let's start with the fundamentals.

It is safe to say that the purpose of any healthcare system should be primarily to improve the health of the population it serves. Although this sounds obvious, the truth is that, in the United States, there is no such clearly delineated mission. Even if there were such a mission, there is no mechanism in our current system to implement the processes it takes to effectively and efficiently carry it out.

One main reason is that there are many different agencies and groups that oversee the various components of our large and complex system. Yet none has the ultimate authority to oversee the delivery of all of these various healthcare services to the entire population.

Take, for example, the HHS. Even though it oversees many components of the American healthcare system, such as regulating food products and new pharmaceutical drugs (FDA), implementing the nation's public health insurance programs (Medicare and Medicaid), preventing the outbreak and spread of diseases (CDC), and funding some of the most important medical research in the world (NIH), it is limited by its government roots and its indirect influence over the private sector. The HHS's government roots make it beholden to political pressures, and its limited influence over the private sector makes any of its actions less effective and slow to take effect. In addition, the HHS secretary is usually a political appointee (it is a cabinet-level position) and rarely has any medical or even public health background.

This deficiency of a unified healthcare agency not only makes it difficult to coordinate a "healthcare mission," but it also makes it hard to gather information about diseases in various communities or to monitor the effectiveness (and side effects) of the therapies and drugs being used. It also makes it more difficult to integrate the recent technical advances and medical innovations the healthcare system infrastructure.

The early years of the twenty-first century have seen exponential growth in research and development of tools directed at helping healthcare providers (including doctors, nurses, and hospitals) deliver more effective and efficient healthcare. One of the most important of these tools has been termed "clinical guidelines," and they have been released by various medical societies in the hope of helping clinicians and healthcare institutions. The concept of guidelines is relatively new in medicine and grew out of a combination of the need to preserve physicians' professional autonomy in the face of administrative pressures and a response to rising healthcare costs.[29] These guidelines are designed to help practitioners make clinical decisions based on the latest medical knowledge.

Most guidelines are compiled by committees of medical experts, who use their knowledge of the medical literature to formulate clinically useful suggestions that can be used in the workup and treatment of various conditions. When there is a gap in the medical literature, the committees often use their clinical experience to express what is termed an "expert opinion" on the subject.

Unfortunately, there are many issues associated with the development and use of these guidelines. One of the most important is the fact that, for many clinical conditions, the medical literature is scant or nonexistent. Part of the reason for this is that most large clinical trials on therapeutic agents are published by groups working with drug or device companies whose main aim is to get their product approved for clinical use. Because of this, the studies often use a limited patient population and might exclude various patient groups (women of childbearing age or patients with other concomitant medical problems are common examples). As a result, guideline committees often have to extrapolate from the published findings to apply the findings to other groups or, literally, make an educated guess. Currently, these educated guesses—or expert opinions—may exceed 50 percent of the recommendations in published guidelines. In addition, conflicting findings of published data complicate the committees' ultimate recommendations.

Not surprisingly, guidelines published by one medical society may sometimes differ or even conflict with guidelines published by others. When there is no adjudicating body to determine which guideline to adopt, there may be significant confusion. In addition, these societies have very little power to influence which additional studies are performed to help resolve the knowledge gaps.

To further complicate things, the guidelines are typically difficult to integrate into clinical practice. There are several reasons for this, but one of the most important is the difficulty of applying guidelines to the patient at the bedside (or on an office exam table). This is because most guidelines do not relate to the way the clinician approaches the patient. And even when the guidelines do create decision diagrams (as many guidelines are now starting to include), it is difficult for the physician to access it at the point of care (the bedside).

Another potential area of improvement in our current healthcare system is the ability to identify patterns of diseases and monitor the effectiveness of therapies. The CDC currently performs disease monitoring, and both the CDC and the FDA conduct response to therapies. Research for effective treatment might be initiated or influenced by the CDC, the FDA, or even the NIH. Not surprisingly, there may be duplication of jurisdiction and the bureaucratic problems that brings.

The collection of data for monitoring diseases (and epidemics), response to therapies, and effectiveness of treatment are all complicated, slow, and expensive. Many studies are developed and funded by pharmaceutical firms or device manufacturers seeking FDA approval for their products, while other data are collected from so-called registries (data collected from patient charts). Still other data are gathered from voluntary and mandatory reports to the CDC or FDA by clinicians regarding a patient with a dangerous disease or the development of unusual medication side effects.

In the absence of a single, integrated process to collect and analyze these data, there is usually a substantial delay in obtaining results, and it is typically a costly process.

The obvious answer to integrating guidelines into clinical practice and obtaining more complete and current health information from around the country is to computerize the process. But, unfortunately, this is an almost impossible task in the current healthcare system.

First, there is no single information platform used by all participants in our current healthcare delivery system. Instead, there is a huge range of computer-based programs in hospitals and medical offices that are used primarily to keep medical records and facilitate billing. Not only are these programs usually ill equipped to integrate practice guidelines, but they also are rarely linked to outside systems. In addition, because there is no "standard" for these programs (which are usually developed as proprietary products), they rarely are able to communicate with one another in any meaningful way.

Second, even if these issues were resolved and an integrated computerized platform was developed, there would still not be an easy way to integrate these guidelines into the current healthcare delivery model. That is because our current healthcare system is overly influenced by the type of insurance coverage (or lack of it) and does not have an agency to coordinate its universal implementation.

EMBRACE's third innovation, the NMB, is set up as the brain and heart of our nation's new healthcare system (see details in chapter 1). Its oversight of all aspects of the healthcare system will not only give it control of healthcare delivery to the entire population, but it will also be able to prioritize which research is needed to make that delivery more effective and efficient. The fully integrated system under EMBRACE and the HIP is developed around the UBF, which facilitates the use of practice guidelines at the point of care and allows for the collection of almost instantaneous epidemiologic data.

This information will be complete (as information from the entire population will be transmitted via the HIP), instantly available for analysis, and inexpensive.

Because the NMB oversees the entire database, it is more readily available for meaningful analysis, and duplication is less likely. The NMB can use the database not only to monitor epidemiologic occurrences and responses to any treatment side effects but also to modify tier assignments and even look for patterns of tier-system abuse.

In addition, because the NMB has control over how the tiers will be allocated, there is ample opportunity to incorporate guidelines into the tier assignments. This is done in a way that does not interfere with clinicians' workflow and allows them to tailor the workup and therapy to the patient's needs. This mechanism of guideline integration into the HIP/UBF also allows for the seamless incorporation of preventive services into the workflow. And because Tier 1 covers all of these preventive and lifesaving services, they will be easily available and free to the consumer/patient.

Other preventive services and programs can also be established under EMBRACE. One such program might include awarding Tier 2 upgrades to patients/consumers who have met several of their treatment goals. For example, those who stop smoking might be awarded Tier 2 coverage as long as they continue to refrain from smoking. Of course, this will have to be verified by some mechanism. Other examples could include weight loss or diabetes control.

Another possible initiative of the EMBRACE system might provide tax exemptions for businesses that develop effective fitness or prevention programs for their employees. Although this might exist now in some corporations, there is no mechanism in our current healthcare system to study the effectiveness of these programs or to compare programs. Under EMBRACE, comparative effectiveness studies will be much easier to conduct because all participants are automatically enrolled in the databases.

Automatic enrollment will be beneficial no matter what public health initiative is undertaken. This will make studies easier to carry out and analyze and will cost significantly less than they do currently.

The most important public health advantage of EMBRACE over the current system, however, is the ability of the NMB to commission studies that will produce data tailored specifically for clinical use in the tiered healthcare system. These large population studies will be easier to organize, significantly less expensive than current studies, and have a built-in infrastructure to translate the data into practice.

The effect of EMBRACE on the nation's healthcare system, and especially the nation's health, would be far-reaching. This is not simply because it assures universal coverage and helps keep healthcare costs under control, which has been the focus of prior healthcare reform efforts. EMBRACE will also significantly emphasize prevention and treatment of the most life-threatening ailments. And, when fully implemented, EMBRACE will have the mechanisms in place not only to develop and implement clinically useful testing protocols and therapies but also to monitor their usefulness, efficiency, and effectiveness in a timely way. In addition, current data will be available on possible new illness outbreaks, which currently might take months or years to identify.

TABLE 8. Comparison of EMBRACE, current, and single-payer systems' features for public health

Public health features	EMBRACE	Current system	Single payer†
Universal coverage	Tier 1: yes	No	Yes*
Access to doctors/hospitals	Unlimited	Limited by insurance coverage	Limited by insurance coverage*
Oversight	Strong	Weak and sporadic	Strong
Ease of integrating guidelines	Built into the system	Difficult	Moderate
Ease of monitoring epidemics	Easy and immediate	Difficult	Moderate
Emphasis on prevention	Strong	Weak	Strong
Ease of data acquisition	Very easy	Hard	Moderate

Note: One must keep in mind that because neither EMBRACE nor an American version of a single-payer system currently exists, some of the claims listed here are best estimations.

† Because one cannot predict which single-payer model might be adopted in the United States, the NHI proposal and/or the Canadian system is used for comparison.

*Almost all single-payer systems in free-market countries have some form of private insurance, which has developed separately from the original single-payer system. There are varying degrees of oversight for these plans. The independent growth of private insurance is likely to occur in the United States as well if a single-payer model is adopted.

28   The Organization for Economic Co-operation and Development (OECD). http://www.oecd.org/els/health-systems/oecdhealthdata2013-frequentlyrequesteddata.htm.
29   George Weisz et al., "The Emergence of Clinical Practice Guidelines," *Milbank Quarterly* 85, no. 4 (2007): 691–727.

Epilogue

How can we make EMBRACE a reality?

As with all healthcare reform initiatives, the first step is to pass legislation in Washington, DC. But unlike the ACA, this legislation does not need to have any of the detailed discussions about insurance or even the Tier Benefits System outlined in this book. Instead, all the energy can be directed toward the creation of the NMB. Once the NMB is created and funded, the NMB itself will take care of implementing the rest of the EMBRACE features.

Much of the complexity of setting up the NMB will be political. This is inevitable, as government involvement in healthcare administration has become so deeply rooted in the American political psyche. But there is precedence for creating such an independent, nongovernment oversight board—namely, the US Federal Reserve, which celebrated its one-hundredth birthday in 2013.

The Federal Reserve was established at a time when US banks had little oversight and operated with an independence that had a deleterious effect on the national economy. It was designed to centrally regulate the banks and US money supply in a way that is independent of direct government control. Similarly, too much government oversight of "public" insurance and not enough oversight of private insurance in our current system have had a detrimental effect that would greatly benefit from an independent agency like the Federal Reserve.

Thus, it appears that the establishment of the NMB has an excellent precedent. It should appeal to both political parties, as long as they are able to overcome special interest groups (also known as lobbyists), such as the drug and medical device companies, who may feel threatened by losing the tremendous influence over healthcare policy that they now enjoy.

This also makes advocating for the EMBRACE system to be established somewhat easier than other healthcare reform legislations. It can be reduced to one goal—namely the creation of an independent National Medical Board. The legislation to create the NMB will also need to address the gradual phasing out of HSS and the VA programs and their integration into the NMB.

Because the NMB will need to be established first and because the other two innovations—the tier system and the HIP—will be easier to implement once an NMB is established, it may be worthwhile to muse on a subsequent timeline for full implementation.

Once the NMB is established, the president will appoint its first chairperson for a ten-year term. This chair will then choose the board members needed to head the NMB's various "departments." These departments will include (but are not limited to) the following:

- Public Health (in place of the CDC)
- Tier Management (responsible for determining the content of each tier and what research is needed to make better determinations)
- Finance (charged with preparing the budget and presenting it to Congress)
- Research (in place of the NIH)
- Pharmaceutical and Device Administration (in place of the FDA)
- Health Information Platform Administration (responsible for development and maintenance of the HIP)
- HealthMart Administration (responsible for developing and overseeing the marketplace for all Tier 2 insurance)
- Medical Education and Maintenance of Certification

- Patient Services
- Business Liaison

There will be only one budget bill presented annually to Congress to cover all of the NMB departments. This budget will not only be easy to understand but also make it easier to control the true amount of healthcare spending.

In addition to the central NMB, EMBRACE will have several regional NMB branches—similar to the twelve branches of the Federal Reserve. These branches will manage the regional differences in both the overall health status and the healthcare delivery that exist across the country.

It will likely be several years before the NMB is ready for the next phase of the EMBRACE rollout: the HIP and the UBF. That is not to say that work will not be done on these web-based programs while the NMB is implemented. In fact, both will be developed parallel to the NMB rollout but will not go live until the NMB is fully functional and all the bugs in the HIP have been resolved.

Even before the HIP goes live, entrepreneurs will be allowed to begin developing software applications that work on the platform and conform to the interconnectivity required. These should include, but are not limited to, apps for EMRs and practice management, as well as for displaying, reading, and reporting medical imaging studies.

The final innovation will be the establishment of the tier system. As with the establishment of the HIP, the NMB will work on the tier system from the beginning so that, as soon as the HIP and the UBF are ready, they can be rolled out. During this time, the NMB will decide which diagnoses go into the three tiers and will work to establish the Tier 2 menu of private insurance choices.

When the tier system is launched, patients will be entered into Tier 1 the first time they visit a medical provider. This could be when the patient is born, sees a doctor in the office, or is admitted to a hospital. The HealthMart will be launched simultaneously to allow consumers the ability to supplement their Tier 1 coverage with Tier 2.

Acronyms

EMBRACE ACRONYMS

EMBRACE: Expanding Medical and Behavioral Resources with Access to Care for Everyone
HIP: Healthcare Information Platform
NMB: National Medical Board
UBF: Universal Billing Form

GENERAL ACRONYMS

ABMS: American Board of Medical Specialties
ACA: Affordable Care Act
CDC: Centers for Disease Control and Prevention
CMS: Centers for Medicare and Medicaid Services
EMR: Electronic Medical Records
FDA: Food and Drug Administration
FICA: Federal Insurance Contributions Act
HHS: Health and Human Services
HMO: Health Maintenance Organization
NHI: National Health Insurance
NIH: National Institutes of Health
VA: Veterans Affairs

www.ingramcontent.com/pod-product-compliance
Lightning Source LLC
Chambersburg PA
CBHW070328190526
45169CB00005B/1788